Etsy Empire

Proven Tactics for Your Etsy Business Success, Including Etsy SEO, Etsy Shop Building, Social Media for Etsy and Etsy Pricing Tips

Eric Michael

Table of Contents

Readers' Praise for Almost Free Money

5.0 out of 5 stars

The author is a money-making machine

By Bill Nelson

This review is from: Almost Free Money: How to Make Extra Money on Free Items That You Can Find Anywhere, Including Garage Sales, Thrift Shops, Scrap Metal and Finding Gold (Kindle Edition)

"This guy is like a money-making machine. Almost Free Money: How to Make Significant Money on Free Items That You Can Find Anywhere, Including Garage Sales, Scrap Metal, and Discarded Items by Eric Michael is yet another goldmine of information on how to make money!

Seriously, whether you want to earn some extra cash in your spare time or want to make a career out of buying and selling, this book (and several others by the same author) will get you going, and keep you there. The appendix is worth the price of the book but every page contains valuable tips and pointers. Highly recommended 5-stars."

5.0 out of 5 stars

This is a great book! It contains lots of ideas on how to make money from surprising places

By Steven Johnson "Publisher of debt and credit"

This review is from: Almost Free Money: How to Make Extra Money on Free Items That You Can Find Anywhere, Including Garage Sales, Thrift Shops, Scrap Metal and Finding Gold (Kindle Edition)

"This is a great book! It contains lots of ideas on how to make money from surprising places, and the resource directory at the back of the book is worth 10x the price of this book all by itself. Highly recommended.

I like the way the author told how he got started in this type of business, and his advice on what to sell as scrap, what to sell as collectible, and what to sell as utilitarian, everyday use, was very interesting. I'm sure that as I visit thrift shops and garage sales in the future, this book will help me identify many new items that will make me money!"

<u>Readers' Praise for Eric Michael's Passive Income for Life</u>

5.0 out of 5 stars **A detailed instruction guide for achieving selling success on Amazon**
By Pete Densmore

"I was hoping this book was going to tell me how to make $50,000 instantly, but I hindsight, I'm very happy it didn't. Because although it's not impossible to make that kind of money quickly, one would either need to be insanely lucky or do something illegal.

Instead, I was pleasantly surprised with Mr. Michael's Passive Income for Life. Like most things in life, making money takes work. It's not something that's handed out on street corners or to those who feel they are entitled. It takes work and it won't happen overnight. That theme is stressed in this book and a theme I will instill with my kids.

Although it will take time, fortunately--with a detailed how-to from Mr. Michael, readers of this book can probably achieve the same success as the author. If they really want it, and if they want to put in the time and effort. The guidance is real and straight forward. The voice is authentic and compassionate. And the feeling is energetic and positive.

If you're looking for supplemental income, a work from home job or starting your own business, I would highly recommend this book. Online success is achievable, with patience, dedication and drive."

Readers' Praise for Almost Free Gold!

5.0 out of 5 stars **Informative and very helpful!**
Sammy K. (Galveston, TX)
This review is from: Almost Free Gold!: How to Earn a Quick $1000 Finding Gold, Silver and Platinum Where You Live (Almost Free Money) (Kindle Edition)

"I have been picking at yard sales and thrift stores for years and have used several of the other books in this series with success, including Almost Free Money. I learned a lot that I didn't know from Almost Free Gold. For me, the most valuable portions of the book were the methods for finding hidden gold and sterling at yard sales.

I've got lots of new places to look and now I know how to find the stuff that other pickers have missed! I am also planning on taking the author's advice and contacting some of the businesses mentioned for setting up consistent sources of precious metals. Plus, you have to check out the chapter on the metal that is more valuable than gold! Fascinating stuff and the basis for a new hobby / business / addiction combination!"

PREFACE

Welcome to the Etsy Empire. This book is the first combination of all aspects of building a successful business on Etsy. In this book, you will learn how to build a shop with built-in demand. You will learn how to convert that demand to sales instantly by providing a premium shopping experience that is offered by only the upper crust of Etsy sellers.

More importantly, you will learn how to engage your customers to develop a fan base of return customers. You will learn about the power of building buzz for your shop by utilizing free marketing tools on social media sites like Pinterest and Facebook.

If you are an experienced Etsy shop owner, you will learn how to enhance the appeal of your shop by building an attractive brand and learning how to communicate with your best fans via email lists and social media.

Since the year 2000, I have sold over 10,000 items that I have "picked" from second-hand locations or have found for free while I was recreating. My search for this information and the resulting business plans for developing fun and exciting income sources at very low costs are detailed in #1 Amazon <u>bestsellers Almost Free Money</u> and <u>Passive Income</u> for Life.

I provide fellow internet sellers over 80 pages of free blog posts on my website at http://www.ericmichaelbooks.com. You can find information on selling a huge array of used items – everything from used media and vintage clothes to scrap metal and everything in between.

I provide this personal resume, if you will, only so that the reader knows where I am coming from when I provide this information. You may be able to find portions of this information (how do you think I learned to do it?) online or in books, but most of this material comes from my personal experiences locating and selling materials and items online. You cannot find most of this information for free, and if you were to try to surf the 'net and put this together, it would take you a very long time.

I have been told that most information providers that sell documents like this book and Almost Free Money charge over $50 for their documents, and actually sell them to customers for that amount. I don't believe in that. I provide this resource to readers for a very affordable charge. In return, all I ask is three things:

1. Leave a positive review on the Amazon book page and on Goodreads.com. The income earned from these books is used for my two boys' college funds.
2. Share this book through your social media outlets and word-of-mouth.
3. Put this information to good use and don't wait to start making money! People who wait for next week usually never end up getting started at all.

Remember, the great thing about Etsy Empire, Almost Free Money and Passive Income for Life is that as soon as you sell that first item, you have already made profit on your book order! Where else can you say that about any investment?

ETSY 101: WHAT IS ETSY.COM AND WHAT CAN I SELL THERE?

Etsy.com describes itself as "the world's most vibrant handmade marketplace". Currently, it hosts a very active community of over 30 million buyers and sellers of hand-made crafts, vintage collectibles and clothing and original creations that can be found nowhere else.

According to Etsy guidelines, only certain types of items can be offered for sale on the website: Handmade creations, vintage items over 20 years old and art supplies.

In addition to providing the ability to market unique wares to an existing market of crafts and vintage goods shoppers, Etsy also allows sellers an excellent opportunity to interact with other people that are interested in their niches and to network effectively with other sellers in their market.

The site caters to artists and crafters. Handmade goods can be offered for sale in a manner that highlights their best features to customers. The photographs are large and items can easily be showcased to customers who are looking to buy similar items.

The average internet shopper knows that Etsy is the place to go for unique creations and home-made crafts. However, there is also a vibrant community of buyers for vintage and "retro" collectibles, clothes and other items on the website. It is an excellent outlet for thrift store and yard sale flippers to sell certain types of goods. That was how I originally became an Etsy seller years ago. While I was learning how to sell online, I offered some unsold eBay auction items on Etsy and was pleasantly surprised when they sold for 3-5 times the value of the eBay opening bid amount.

As we progress into this book, we will discuss what types of goods sell well on Etsy and you will learn how to set up your shop to maximize profit and internet traffic. We will also talk about how to use social media sites like Pinterest and Facebook to broaden your reach and bring you more customers from the internet.

Anybody can learn how to sell on Etsy! Even if you have no prior internet selling experience, you can set up a shop and start selling items quickly. In this book, we will walk you through the process and get you started selling. If you are already an Etsian, we will provide you with new and profitable ideas for organizing your shop, gaining more returning customers and creating more profitable items for your shop.

Owning an Etsy shop can be a rewarding experience and it can also be very profitable, if your store is designed properly. We will go through the steps that are necessary to follow to become a successful Etsy shop owner.

Who Shops on Etsy?

Before we decide on what we are going to sell on Etsy, it is important to understand who we are going selling our goods to.

According to Alexa.com, female users on the site are "greatly over-represented", compared to the general population of internet users. In a 2012 case study (admittedly somewhat dated, but Etsy's demographic numbers are not published anywhere), some important trends were noted. Females represented 67% of the users on the site – a huge majority. "Visitors ages 18-34 accounted for 43% of the total visitors. In addition, 88% were Caucasian, 69% had no children, and 48% earned under $60,000/year. Interestingly, 62% have a college education under their belt. What does this mean? A typical Etsy.com potential customer is an 18 to 34 year old college-educated white female with no children, who makes less than $60,000/year."

It seems like the user population has diversified recently as the site has matured (it is still a fairly young site - launched in 2005), but it is still important to realize who your primary target population is.

Eric Michael

The Best Selling Shops on Etsy

Want to get an idea of what sells on Etsy and how the big fish are killing it on Etsy? Check out the top 100 sellers by clicking on the link below.

http://www.handmadeology.com/top-100-handmade-etsy-sellers-july-2013

According to CraftCount, which tracks the best-selling Etsy shops, the entire top 10 in the 'supply shops' category in mid-2012 sold jewelry findings and/or beads.

The hand-made category was more diverse: #1 was a maker of comic buttons, #2 and #9 were makers of soaps, #3 sold paper curios, dolls and children's art, #4 sold flat stamps and botanical prints, #5 sold fun shirt and bags for the family, #6 sold vintage prints with animals dressed as people, #7 sold original animal prints on dictionary pages, #8 sold soaps and body lotions and #10 sold Scrabble tile jewelry and décor.

The vintage category top 10 is even more eclectic. Among the top 10 are sellers of vintage prints, jewelry pieces and findings, vintage furniture hardware and supplies, vintage clothing, vintage watch parts and findings and several general thrift shop resale shops.

What does this all mean? You can make a lot of money selling a wide variety of shop inventories on Etsy. The most important thing is to build your brand and have your own identity. Of course, it helps to know ahead of time that there is an existing demand for what you would like to sell. It also helps to sell to the majority of the customers on Etsy, which we have already established to be heavily weighted toward the young female demographic. It is important to market your shop to the majority and know what people are already buying.

Research, people. Research.

PREPARE TO SUCCEED ON ETSY

Before we set up our shops on Etsy, there are some very important tasks that must be accomplished, or you will be setting yourself up for failure.

It's important to understand that many Etsy sellers make $1000 a month, or less. That's $12,000 a year. According to several case studies, Etsy sellers that considered themselves full-time sellers earned just under $49,000, which is not bad for doing what you love to do. However, this is not a quick road to wealth. It is entirely possible to make six figures selling on Etsy. There are a number of very successful shops that earn well over $100,000.

But, for every one shop that makes $100K, there are thousands that only earn several thousand a year.

I'll get to my point. If you want to be one of the ultra-successful Etsy shop owners, you will have to work harder and smarter than your competitors. You will have to spend hours of time doing research to be successful and you will have to understand your customers and competition. You will have to run your Etsy shop like a true business to get a leg up on other similar shops.

If you are only looking to earn some spending money or pay for your groceries each month, that's OK, too. Perhaps you just want to get your art, crafts, or vintage treasure out in the public eye. That is another goal of many beginning Etsy sellers. Usually, after you make your first couple of sales or you sell that first $50 creation, you start thinking, "Hey, I could make a lot more money than what I originally thought."

Then, you are hooked.

Step One: Set Realistic Goals for Your Etsy Business

I have seen a number of Etsy success plans in books that give you a 7-step or 10-step plan for success. They all talk about the importance of setting goals, but some of them recommend learning how to navigate on the Etsy marketplace first.

In my opinion, the most important thing that you must decide as a businessperson is what your goals are going to be. These goals will affect everything else that comes afterward. They are going to direct you in the amount of time that you are going to spend researching items to sell, how much time and money that you are going to spend on inventory and how much you spend on initial expenses.

Most successful Etsy shop owners have goals that are financial or inventory-based. Why? Because they are the only measurable numbers that Etsians have to set attainable goals. A goal that states "I want to have a popular shop" or "I want to be able to quit my second job at the restaurant" are not measurable goals.

Your goals must include tangible numbers. In the first full month of selling, your goal may be to completely set up your Etsy shop and sell $100 worth of goods. That is an attainable goal. The next month, your goals may be to have 50 items in your shop inventory and have $300 in sales.

Goals keep you moving forward and growing as a businessperson. It's also important to set both short-term and long-term goals. The short-term goals keep you focused on day-to-day tasks, while your long-term goals should allow you to develop your business plan over time to achieve your goals. Just make sure that you keep your goals attainable.

An Etsy business is similar to any other business outside of the internet. It takes a while to get to the point where you are consistently making money. You are going to have to put in some time and money to get there. Success is not going to happen overnight for 99% of Etsy sellers. There are going to be some lean months at the beginning.

It's good to dream big, but you don't want to continually come up short. It feels great to achieve your long-term goals!

Step Two: Familiarization with the Etsy Marketplace

Now that we have a set of goals set for our business, we will move on to understanding how Etsy works.

Before you can develop a shop that attracts a lot of customers, you must first figure out who your customers are going to be and how they will find your shop from the Etsy website. Later, we will discuss how customers can use search engines to find your shop. In this chapter, we will talk about how customers use Etsy to find the goods that they want to buy.

If you are a frequent customer on Etsy, you can skip this portion of the chapter and go to the next subtitle. If not, let's go shopping!
Our goal for this session is to become familiar with the website. Look around, go into some interesting shops, click on items and look at how Etsy displays goods and shops to entice customers.

Let's go into the Etsy website: https://www.etsy.com. Doesn't Etsy do a fabulous job of showcasing artisans right from the welcome page? eBay doesn't do that on their welcome page. Etsy puts a focus on its sellers and their relationships with consumers of crafts and vintage goods. You will also notice that Etsy's welcome page is marketed towards women – there are photographs of women and shops with women's names featured. This is another reminder to make your business attractive to women as we develop our shops.

Now, it is possible to wander around Etsy without creating a profile, but in order to buy anything, customers have to log in and create a profile. Let's do that now. Click on the 'Sign In' link at the top right corner of the page. Enter your information and connect your account to your Paypal account. If you do not have a Paypal account, you will be provided a link to sign up for Paypal. It will be necessary to accept Paypal payments to sell on Etsy as 95% of your customers will pay with Paypal.

You can also link your profile to your Facebook page, so that you can log in through your Facebook page, with a click of a button. We will talk more about connecting social media to your Etsy shop later.

OK. Now that you have a profile, you are ready to shop. The profile that you set up will also eventually be connected to your Etsy selling shop. Both your buying and selling on Etsy are done under the same profile. You do not have to set up your shop when you first register for Etsy as a customer. You don't even have to name your shop yet, and that's good. We have to do some research before we get to the point that we are ready to build your shop.

Let's do an exercise in Etsy marketplace navigation. We will refer back to this later, so please follow along. Let's locate something that we want to buy and purchase it on Etsy! This exercise is both fun and practical research for developing our shop. You have to first experience the site as a customer to be able to tailor your shop to entice your own customers to buy items from your shop.

So, let's say that I want to buy a vintage clock for my retro home office. That would be cool, right? The 1960s had some awesome clocks with vibrant colors and unique designs.

There are several ways that I can find what I am looking for from the Etsy home page. I am not the type of shopper who wants to look around for an hour. I want to find what I want to buy and get on with my day. So, I would simply type in a query on the search bar at the top of the page. We will discuss the Etsy search engine in detail later in the Etsy SEO chapter, but for now, just understand that the more keywords that you type into the search bar, the fewer results that you will get back to look at and the narrower the variance in items will be.

You can also narrow your search by using the 'minus' key. For instance, I might type in 'wall clock retro, –wood' because I do not want to buy a wood clock. Notice that as you type in your search query, a drop-down box appears below the search bar. The drop-down contains suggested searches that are popular with Etsy shoppers. You can either click on the drop-down suggestions, or type your own complete query and hit the return key to display your search returns. Unless your query was very detailed, you will see hundreds or thousands of items displayed. You can already get an idea of how important it is going to be for you to enter item titles with effective keywords when you start selling your own items.

Now, click on the orange Etsy button and return to the home page. Another way that shoppers will find your goods is by browsing in the categories provided on the welcome page. I would click on the 'Vintage' category to find my clock. From that page, you can scan down and see that the most popular items have their own sections with large photographs displayed on the main category page. Clocks are not one of these choices, so I click on 'Home Décor' from the main category list.

From there, it is possible to browse a large selection of décor items, until I find a clock (or something else that I like better). I could have also found clocks in several other categories, including 'Antiques' and 'Collectibles'. Note that you can sort by price and shop location at the top of the page. You can also always choose to default back to the search bar at the top of the page, if you get tired of browsing through hundreds of items.

Let's pick out a clock that we like. Again, note how the items are displayed in the showcase photographs and look at the keywords provided in the title. I picked out a cool looking starburst-style clock.

When you 'mouse over' an item (point at it with your cursor/arrow/finger), several options appear. You can click on the whole item and continue on to the item detail page. You can also click on the 'heart' to mark the item as a favorite or the 'list' to add the item to a specific list that you can set up for specific categories of items. We will also discuss these options in-depth later. Another option is to click on the 'Pin It' button to pin the item's image to a Pinterest board. This is a great feature for Etsy shop owners, as many people buy Etsy items directly from Pinterest. We will also develop strategies for using Pinterest for your shop in subsequent chapters.

I decide that this starburst clock is the one that I want for my office, so I click through to the item description page. In the item page, I am provided more details about the item and up to four additional photographs. There is a ton of other links that Etsy provides to help sellers sell their items from the detail page. The same 'mouse-over' options are available here – you can favorite the item or add it to a list. You can also post the item to Facebook or Twitter, in addition to Pinterest. You can Favorite the shop, ask the shop owner a question about the item or shop and see some other related items in the sellers' shop. Notice that at the bottom of the page, you are provided with tabs for selecting keywords in the 'Related to the Item' section. These keywords are selected by the seller during the listing process. Remember how these are displayed, so that we can talk about them later.

Having looked at the clock's item page, I liked what I saw. I checked the other 4 photos and did not see any damage. I read the description and the seller seems to know what they are talking about. I decide to purchase the clock, so I continue to 'Add to Cart' to pay for the item.

From the payment page, you have several options for payment, including entering your credit card information or using Paypal. There is also the option to add a note to the shop owner. If you add a note, Etsy provides that message to the seller in an email. You also see several rows of items underneath the payment box, where other clocks are displayed in the 'People who purchased your item, also bought…' section. Etsy will try to upsell additional items from your shop (or others' shops) with every purchase.

After I enter my payment via Paypal, Etsy sends me an email about the item, along with shipping information. You are also directed to a page that allows you to brag about the item that you found to your friends on social media.

What did we learn with this exercise? We learned that having great item titles and photographs are vital. We also learned that Etsy does a terrific job of integrating shops and items with social media and networking options, so that each purchase provides multiple opportunities to upsell additional items.

Another location that is vital to spend some time before launching your shop is on the Etsy Community (Link at top of page). Here you can pick up a wealth of information from other Etsy sellers. Check out the forums to read about how sellers have solved particular problems, built their shops and handled customers. You could easily spend an entire day or two absorbing information in the forums and you can come back later and make some important contacts with other sellers.

Etsy Circles is another must-see location. Etsy Circles are groups of sellers that are involved in particular categories. Many circles are also sub-divided by location. For instance, there are Steampunk circles for many individual states in the US. Find several circles in categories that you are considering selling in. You can read the posts in many circles and see what sellers are talking about. You may choose to bookmark several circles and come back to apply after you open your shop. You must be accepted to post in a circle, but you can view any discussions that are marked Public.

The Etsy Blogs should be your last stop, because it is going to be important to remember what you learn there. Under the Blogs tab are links to the Etsy Blog, Etsy News Blog and the Seller Handbook. You may wish to scan the News Blog and see what is going on, but the Seller handbook is the real reason that we are looking at this tab.

The handbook contains dozens of outstanding articles for both beginning and experienced Etsians. The articles are provided by the Etsy staff. They focus on providing tips to organize your business, price goods and develop your brand. Before I built my shop, I read all of the applicable posts in the Handbook. There is a lot of information that can help you to develop a profitable business on Etsy.

There are two final pages to visit:

1) Etsy Seller Guidelines at https://www.etsy.com/help/article/4507

2) Etsy Seller FAQs at https://www.etsy.com/help/topics?ref=help_faq_suggestion

Step Three: Etsy Market Research – How to Make Your Shop a Guaranteed Winner!

As we have discussed in previous chapters, it is important to treat your Etsy business just like any other business outside of the internet. As such, the research that you conduct before launching your business will ensure that your Etsy shop will be profitable and successful in the future.

Think of it this way – would you build a shop in a city that you had never been to without finding out if people would go to your new store if it were built? Would you pay to load your shelves in your new shop with goods for sale without determining whether people in that town buy those types of goods? Of course you wouldn't! You would talk to people that live where you want to build the store first and find out if there is an existing demand for your products.

This is a mistake that limits many new Etsy shops and it is the main reason why these shops only make a couple of hundred dollars (or less) each month. There are tons of shops on Etsy that were haphazardly built with no advance planning. There are many more shops that were built only to sell a small selection of products that have insufficient demand to allow for business growth.

Many artists and crafters already have decided everything that they are going to sell before they build their Etsy shop. That is a mistake! It is almost impossible to generate a large-scale additional demand for products after they are already for sale. It is substantially easier to make products that customers are already looking to buy than it is to try to entice customers into buying new types of goods.

Think about your own buying habits. How many times have you gone on an internet marketplace (eBay, Etsy, or Amazon, for example) looking to buy a product and bought something completely different on a whim? Sometimes it happens, but that is not normal consumer behavior.

This is the most important thing to remember when building your shop: SELL GOODS THAT PEOPLE ALREADY WANT TO BUY!

Say it with me again. SELL STUFF THAT PEOPLE ALREADY WANT TO BUY.

Seems like common sense, doesn't it? Yet, thousands of Etsians are trying to jam a square peg into a round hole by attempting to build a totally new consumer group for their goods instead of selling goods to existing buyers that are already buying a particular type of goods.

Does that mean that you can't sell unique creations or your own original line of clothing? Of course not! That's what makes Etsy great. What it means is that we are going to find a way to market your unique art to an existing group of consumers. Get traffic to your shop and then you can sell shoppers whatever you want, as long the items are consistent with what those consumers would expect to see in your shop.

The question then becomes: How do I know what people want to buy?

There are two easy ways to determine demand for Etsy products:

1) **Etsy Demand**
2) **Google search engine results**
3) **Craftcount.com**

1) Obviously, the sales of existing items on Etsy will be the most accurate predictor of how your own items will sell. After all, these customers are already shopping on Etsy and they like the same types of goods that you may be offering from your own shop. However, Etsy

does not offer sellers the ability search site-wide completed sales, like eBay does.

Instead, Etsy sellers have to infer sales by examining a selection of shops in their categories. On the left side of each Shop home page, there is a link for sales. The link includes the number of sales for the shop. You might see a '1,113 sales' hyperlink. If you click on that link, you will see a list of the sold items for that individual shop. You can sort the list by 'Most Recent' or 'Most Sales'.

It is frustrating for many sellers that it is impossible to see the values of the items that were sold, but Etsy sellers have campaigned several times to keep it that way. You can get a good idea of the type of items that are selling well in multiple shops and you can also navigate into the shops existing listings to look at the cost of current active listings. The Etsy search bar can also tell you what customers are shopping for on the website, which is also great information to have at your fingertips. There are several ways to go about collecting this information.

The first method is to start typing in each letter of the alphabet to look at the drop-down box search returns. If you type in 'a', you get a drop-down list of 13 search terms, which are the most popular searches performed by Etsy customers that contain the letter 'a' in one word of the search. If you click on a link in the drop-down you are provided a search return, with a number of items listed on Etsy with that group of words in the title, category or tag. For instance, if you type in 'a' and then click on the top term 'Wall Art', you get over 800K returns.

You can go through the entire alphabet to get an idea of what search terms customers are typing into the search bar.

Another way to use the search bar to your benefit is to type in a one or two word phrase associated to what you may be selling. If you type in 'clock' into the search bar, you will see that 'unique wall clocks' is the most popular term that is actually typed into the search bar. I found that surprising. I would have thought that 'Wall Clock' or 'Alarm Clock' would have been the top search term. That's exactly why you conduct this type of research!

How can this information help us? Well, the obvious answer is that you now know that if you sell clocks, you would get a lot of traffic by including 'Unique wall clock' in your item title and description. Perhaps you might also decide to design your entire shop around that search term and include 'Unique Wall Clocks' in your shop title, or at least have that term in your shop description, which is read by Etsy and Google search engines.

I would suggest that you conduct this type of drop-down research for any terms that might be associated with your shop. Write down each term from the drop-down in order, along with the number of items that return from each Etsy search.

Isn't this awesome information to have before you design your shop?! Before you even start designing your shop, you know the most popular items and shops that customers are looking for on Etsy. You can design your shop to market your goods toward the most popular search terms. You can include a number of popular search terms in your store description, which will bring you instant traffic from the Etsy search engine. You can make items (or find vintage items) to put in your store that will bring you traffic. You can put popular keywords in your item titles and descriptions, which will bring you more shoppers who will be looking to buy your goods!

2) Google Adwords Keyword Planner:
https://adwords.google.com/ko/KeywordPlanner/Home
Etsy shops and items can also get significant traffic from search engines outside of Etsy and Google is used more often than all of the other search engines put together. The Google Adwords Keyword Planner is a great tool. It allows you type in search terms and see how many people Googled that term in the last month, along with the competition for each term.

In order for search terms to be useful for your shop, you should look for two or three word keyword phrases. Using single words like 'steampunk' would be useless for your shop, due to the huge number of Google searches for that broad keyword.

To use the Keyword Planner, you must create an Adwords account and sign in. Then, click on 'Search for New Keyword…'. You can type in a group of related keywords, or just type in one keyword at a time. After you generate the suggestions, click on the 'Keyword Ideas' tab at the top of the page.

You will see your keyword at the top of the list, along with the number of monthly Google searches and the competition level (low, medium or high). Below that, you will see a number of related keyword phrases that Google suggests. These additional search terms should be noted, along with the number of searches and the competition level. You can then go back to the query page and type in the refined search term to get additional suggestions.

Ideally, you should be seeking keyword phrases that are low or medium competition and have an adequate number of monthly searches. A keyword that is only searched a hundred times a monthly may not be ideal for a shop title keyword, but it could be great for an item title. Aim for a selection of related keywords with a variety of monthly search numbers. Your most important keywords may end up being three or more word long-tail keyword phrases that few Googlers use, but your shop ends up being the top search return for those phrases on Google.

3) Craftcount.com is another great place to look at successful Etsy shops and see what has made them successful (besides the owners'

hard work). In order to be listed on CC, a shop must have over 1,000 individual sales over the life of the shop. Once your shop hits 1,000 sales, you can register on CC to be included in their lists. This is another source of traffic to your shop.

http://craftcount.com/information.php

What can CC tell us about Etsy demand? It can tell us is which categories on Etsy are top sellers. For instance, from the CC home page, click on the 'Top Sellers by Category' link. Let's say that we want to know which homemade items sell. We click on the 'Homemade' subcategory and then 'Bags and Purses'. CC tells us that there are over 200 sellers in that subcategory that have 1,000 sales. There are also 16 shops with over 10K sales and a top seller of over 37K.

'Bags and Purses' is a subcategory that other sellers have sold in successfully. There is quite a bit of competition there, but if you developed your own niche in that category, you could make some money.

Now look at the 'Miniatures' subcategory (doll furniture, etc.). Here, there are only 27 shops on the list and only two shops with over 10K sales. You might have some tougher sledding in this category, in order to get to 1000 sales.

Another way that CC can help you is by clicking through to shops that will likely be your competitors. Look at their shops and take notes. Look at their items and see how many times they are marked as favorites by shoppers. Find out how many Admirers their shop has. You can get a feel for how their customers interact with the shop and how popular their shops are among Etsy shoppers.

DESIGNING AN ETSY SHOP: TRAFFIC + DEMAND + PROFESSIONALISM = PROFIT

Let's get ready to sell some handmade items or vintage treasures! Most Etsians are creative individuals, so designing a great Etsy store will be right up your alley.

Your main goal for designing your shop is to create a location that your customers will want to return to and shop. If you can create a unique niche that is a cool spot with unique items, your customers will be much more likely to return. It also helps with return traffic if your customers identify with you and your creative process, if you offer handmade items, or how you obtain your collectibles and goods if you sell vintage items.

It should be a lot of fun designing your shop. Don't sweat the small stuff! Let's roll!

Etsy Shop Name: Don't Rush...

Your shop name is very important. Take your time and come up with a good one. Once you decide on a name, you will not want to change it. Your shop name will be on your professionally designed banner and your past customers will be searching for your original shop name in Etsy and Google search engines.

So, what makes for a great Etsy shop name? You have to think like a customer, here. What does a shopper want in a shop name? It has to be easy to remember and easy to spell. Don't try to get creative and use a shop name that has a weird spelling of a common word like using 'Kats', or 'Catz', instead of 'Cats. You want people to be able to type your shop name into a Google search bar and find it immediately.

Your Etsy shop name will also be your internet URL address.
Some other helpful ideas for a profitable shop name:

1. Incorporate a high-ranking Google and Etsy search engine keyword phrase from your research for additional traffic to your shop!
2. Don't make your shop name more than three words. It's too hard to remember.
3. Check Google to make sure that your potential shop name is not copyrighted or trademarked.
4. Check Etsy to ensure that your potential shop name is not already used by another seller, or is very close to the name of an existing shop. If you want to use 'Unique Wall Clocks', make sure there is not an existing shop titled 'Unique Wall Clock'.

5. Consider your target market and come up with a name that will resonate with them. Remember, Etsy shoppers are primarily younger women.

6. Remember that your shop name will be featured in your shop banner and also may be used on your website and/or social media headers. If the title lends itself to a cool banner design, so much the better!

7. Keep it on the straight-and-narrow. Don't try to sound cool. There will be older Etsy shoppers that may be put off by certain shop names. Don't alienate any user groups with your shop name.

8. Alliteration or rhyming can help customers remember your shop name. Amusing plays on words and humor can also be effective.

9. Your shop name has to be one word, so use capital letters to separate words so that they are readable. 'UniqueWallClocks'.

Designing Your Shop Banner

Your shop's banner is the first thing that customers are going to see when looking at your shop. It is extremely important that your banner sets a professional tone for your shop.

The first big step that you can take to establish yourself as a serious Etsy seller is to have a professional designer create a great banner for your shop. You don't have to spend much money at all to have a great banner designed!

There are many gigs on www.Fiverr.com, where professional designers will make you a sharp looking banner for $5. You can also pay a bit more and have a more experienced designer create a banner for $25-50. Google 'Etsy banner design' and you will get a number of websites to explore.

Etsy's banner requirements are as follows: 760 x 100 Pixels, with a resolution of 72 dpi (dots per inch). The image file must be in .jpg, .png., or .gif format.

To make a long story short, DO NOT try to save a buck and make your own banner, unless you are a graphic designer. Nothing says 'amateur' like a crappy shop banner. You can find some very good designers on Fiverr, and if you don't like the design that they create for you, it is easy to get a refund and try another designer. I use Fiverr for many tasks in my business and have been very satisfied with 98% of the results.

Some additional banner tips:

1. Make sure that your shop title is the primary point of interest in the banner. Don't use so many gaudy graphics and background noise that your shop name is hard to read.

2. Use colors and designs that accent your shop inventory. If you are selling doll clothes, pastel colors may be preferable. If you are selling vintage computer parts, a vintage tech-style font may be cool.

3. I have seen several banners that incorporate an arrow that points down at your Facebook Like link on the left side of the banner. This encourages people to click on the Like link.

4. Take a look at some of your competitor's banners and take notes on what you like and don't like. Provide this information to your banner designer when you order.

Designing your Avatar

Your avatar is the small photograph that is displayed in multiple locations on Etsy, including in your shop and item descriptions. Most Etsy sellers either use a photograph of themselves or a photograph that is consistent with their banner art.

In order to upload an Avatar, go to 'Your Account' and then 'Profile'. Click on the 'Browse' button to upload a photo from your computer. Your avatar is a square image that is 75 pixels wide. Etsy will resize images, but an image that is already square may prevent blurring.

Your avatar should be used to develop your shop's brand. Keep the avatar consistent in style and color to your banner, unless you opt to use your image as your avatar. You may also ask your banner's designer to suggest an avatar image. Many designers will do this free of charge. Often, you can use a portion of the banner itself as an avatar, by cropping it with Photoshop and saving it as a new .jpg file.

Adding a Shop Title

Your shop's title is basically a slogan that adds descriptive text to your shop name. If your shop name is 'Unique Wall Clocks', your shop title might be "Vintage Clocks for any Retro style Decor".

You can have up to 66 characters in your shop title and the characters can be letters or numbers. The title can be found in 'Your Account', 'Info and Appearance'. The title is searchable by Google and Etsy search engines, so it is advisable to add some of your keyword phrases from your research to enhance the likelihood of gaining additional traffic to your shop.

Designing an Etsy Shop Announcement

The shop announcement appears in your Etsy shop immediately below your shop banner. The announcement allows you to add more refinement to your title and shop name.

You will see a wide variety of uses for the announcement, if you visit a variety of shops. Some owners use the announcement for advertising upcoming sales. Some owners have a short description of their inventory and philosophy in their announcement. I have also seen sellers describe why they started their Etsy shop, or how they design their creations.

You can use a simple announcement or "go for the gusto" and create a complete profile for your shop that creates a buzz for your items. You can add professionalism by providing several blurbs from interviews that you have done or excellent customer reviews from your buyers.

Here is an excellent announcement from a high-end jewelry shop:

https://www.etsy.com/shop/CatherinetteRings?ref=sr_gallery_11&ga_search_query=steampunk+jewelry&ga_ship_to=US&ga_ref=auto9&ga_search_type=all&ga_view_type=gallery

It contains: Where the seller's rings have been featured in national magazines, an Etsy business timeline, shipping and restocking policies, an 'About Me' for the artist, reservation instructions and 'Press and Events'.

The announcement does get truncated to two short lines, so most of the announcement message will not be seen unless the customer clicks on it. Put your most important statement at the top of your announcement.

Adding to Your Shop Profile and Shop Policies

Your profile details are provided in your shop on the left side of the page. This is another good location to add your bio. You can use this to develop a rapport with your buyers and establish professionalism. Shipping, sales tax and return policies can also be specified.

Other details that can be added: Name, Location, Gender, Birthday, Favorite Materials, Favorite Items.

You can add where you graduated from college, your techniques for designing artwork and your personal interests and influences.

Your profile can be edited from 'Your Account' > 'Public Profile'. Before you submit your profile, make sure that you review your work and spell-check it. Remember, your profile is a direct reflection of you and your business.

Your Etsy shop should also specify its policies, so that customers know what to expect from you. Well-written shop policies help to instill customer confidence. They also prevent negative feedbacks for your shop.

To add your shop policies: Click on your Shop hyperlink at top right > Info and Appearance > Policies (tab at top of page).

There are link tabs to your policies and shipping from both your main shop page and each item sales page. Stores that have no policies are at a disadvantage, because many buyers will be hesitant to order from sellers that they do not trust.

Shop policies do not only help your customers but they also help the shop owner to stay consistent and have actions in place for certain situations.

Here are some things to consider when writing your store policies.

Welcome

Make shoppers feel welcome in your shop and excited to see your creations or goods. A brief introduction is fine and you can encourage buyers to contact you if they have any questions.

I have seen a number of shops that also include how shoppers can determine what size they need to order, what variations are available of their items, and how items are made (if sellers are selling handmade items that are also available in stores).

Payment

State what methods of payment you accept. A brief description of how to pay with Paypal is useful. Many people don't realize they can use this method to pay with their credit or debit card without having to sign up for a Paypal account. It helps to explain how they can do this. This is what I say in my policies, you can copy and paste it if you want

"You do not need a Paypal Account to pay for your items through Paypal.

Choose the Paypal Option during checkout. After you submit your order click the "Pay Now" button. Scroll Down and you will see the option to pay with a Credit or Debit Card without having to sign up for a Paypal account."

State that you will not send packages until payments have cleared.

Tell your buyers what you will do in the event of non-payment. Non-payment is a common problem on Etsy, part of this is due to the way the system works there and it can be confusing to new buyers on Etsy. Other times people are just messing with you.

Will you leave negative feedback for non-payment and no-response to emails? Whatever you decide to do, include it in your policies. It will make it easier for you to follow through when non-payment happens to you.

If you offer payment plans explain how this works to your customers.

SHIPPING

Describe how your items are packaged: Do you gift wrap? Are your items sent in boxes? Do you include a certificate of authenticity? If you use recycled packaging, write that in here, too. Etsy buyers love sellers who do this.

Tell your buyers which shipping companies that you use – USPS, UPS, FedEx. What shipping speeds do you offer? (Priority, standard, first class, registered mail, online tracking?). Can customers request faster shipping or insurance for an additional charge? If yes, ask them to contact you for more information.

If the Etsy and Paypal shipping addresses you receive for an order are different, what will you do? Some stores state if they have had no contact from the buyer within 3 working days, they will ship to the Paypal shipping address. Other sellers clearly state that they always ship to the address given during Etsy checkout. Decide which you will do and state it here.

Give information on estimated shipping times. If you have already done a lot of shipping you will have a good idea of how long a package takes to arrive in certain parts of the world. If you have not done much shipping yet, ask at your post office, and then add a few days to their estimated times. Packages almost always take longer to arrive than the post office says they will. If you ship overseas, state that customs can delay packages by up to 6 weeks. This does not happen often, but it can happen.

Refunds and Exchanges
This is one policy that should be very clear to customers. Careful buyers will look at your return policy quite often before they buy from you. Make sure that you spell out exactly how you handle requests for returns and exchanges.

If you are going to offer refunds and/or exchanges, then put your terms and conditions in this box. How long after receiving an item can people ask you for an exchange or refund? Will you refund only the cost of the item or the shipping as well? If a buyer returns an item to you, who is responsible for the return postal costs?

I strongly recommend that you allow refunds and returns for most items that you sell. You will have some unscrupulous shoppers that will buy handmade goods, just to see how they were made and then return them for a refund. But, you will earn many more sales by accepting returns, so it will more than offset the few refunds that you will issue on fraudulent returns.

Additional Policies and FAQ's

This is a great place for any custom order policies you have. If you take custom orders, you can talk about the process you go through for these orders.

I recommend you at least take a deposit before starting work. Unforeseen things can happen that may mean your buyer cannot pay you by the time you have finished working.

- If you have some questions that you are frequently getting asked, include the questions and your answer to them in the FAQs.
- Run your policies through a spell checker, and get someone else to proof-read them for you if you can. It looks unprofessional if you have spelling and grammar mistakes everywhere.
- Keep a friendly and polite tone in your policies. Be clear and concise without being rude.
- Re-read your policies as if they belonged to a shop you wanted to buy from. How would you feel as the customer when reading them?

- Sometimes people will write to you with questions about your policies. When this happens, take note and make adjustments to your policies if necessary.
- Invite shoppers to interact with you at your social media pages and your blog.

Here is an example of a very effective shop policy page:

https://www.etsy.com/shop/TheHouseOfMouse/policy

Connecting your Facebook and Twitter accounts to Etsy

In order to connect your Etsy shop to your social media pages, go to Your Account > Settings. Then, click on the Facebook and Twitter links to connect them to your Etsy shop. The process is easy and takes only seconds. Adding your social links does several things for you.

1. Establishes even more professionalism for your business. All established businesses have a social media presence. This is even truer if you have a large number of Likes and Follows. Many Etsy sellers buy likes and follows on Fiverr.com for their social media pages.
2. Allows for a one-click Twitter follow or Facebook Like to build your following.

3. Builds customer loyalty, if they can interact with you on your social pages.

4. Allows you to post your new listings on your Facebook and/or Twitter pages with one click. This is awesome, especially on Twitter.

There. Now you have the initial setup completed for your new Etsy shop. Congratulations!

If you completed all of the tasks that we discussed, your Etsy shop will be more professional than over half of the shops on Etsy. That gives you an instant advantage over your competition.

PRICING ETSY ITEMS

Now that we have gotten our Etsy shop set up and looking sharp, we're ready to start making some money, right? Well... almost.

Before we start adding items to our Etsy inventory, we should do some additional research on how we will price items in our Etsy shop. The reason that we conduct that research first is that your pricing strategy will effect what types of items are offered in your shop. The pricing strategy will also guide you when you create your crafts and artwork, if you will be selling handmade items.

For many Etsians, item pricing is the most challenging aspect of selling on Etsy. You want to make the maximum profit on your inventory items, but you don't want to have to pay to relist a bunch of items because they are too expensive. Effective pricing takes practice. The more items that you sell, the easier it becomes to set prices based on your past experiences.

For the first couple of months, you may wish to keep a journal or spreadsheet that shows how much you initially listed your item for, how long it took to sell, and if you had to adjust the price or re-list at a lower price.

You should take the inventory item that you think will sell most often and use that item for your price analysis. Once you have determined the price point for your most popular item, you can use that information to price your other items by comparing them to that item. Are your other items more detailed, or rarer? Do other items take longer for you to make, or are the materials used more expensive? If so, you should price those items higher than your most popular item.

There are three methods for determining a price point for your item:

1. Trial and Error: This is the method that we have already discussed. List items for what you think they are worth and see how quickly they sell. If they don't sell for months, you may wish to lower your price. If it sells almost immediately, you probably underpriced your item. This method works for many items, but keep in mind that some high-priced items may only appeal to relatively few buyers. These types of items can take a while for the right person to come along and find them.

2. Polling: This method is simply asking people what they think the item is worth and taking an average of those prices quoted. There are a number of ways to poll people. Your goal is to find non-biased people to ask about your items. You can ask friends and family, but what do you think that they are going to tell you about pricing your items? Right. They are going to give you inflated prices because they don't want to offend you. You

can join a Facebook group for Etsy sellers or auction sellers. Join an Etsy circle or group. Post your poll in these groups, along with a photo of your item. Ask them what they would expect to pay for that item on Etsy (maybe you will even sell an item or two by asking about them in these locations!).

3. eBay Comparison: eBay can be a great way to establish a price point, as all auctions listed will end at a certain price. It's even better if you can re-list several examples of the same item and then take an average price. This is the best method to price unique art and high-end craft items. You might be very surprised at how much people are willing to pay for these types of items! On the flip-side, you may have thought that your crafts would garner lots of bids and end at a higher price than what eBay bidders tell you. Just keep in mind that Etsy shoppers are usually shopping for home-made items or vintage items, so you may wish to list your item on Etsy at a slightly higher price point than what your eBay auctions end up selling for.

Effective Price Point Strategies

Before we start talking about actual numbers for our price points, we must first establish our break-even point. This is not as easy as it may first appear, and that is why some Etsy sellers end up losing money on their transactions.

The first aspect of cost is easy to determine. How much did it cost you to buy your vintage item at a second-hand store? How much did the materials cost to make the handmade item?

The second aspect of cost is also usually factored into price points by Etsy shop owners, as well. What are the fees going to cost you when the item sells on Etsy? Both Etsy and Paypal charge fees for each transaction. Etsy charges 3.5% of your sales price for closing costs per transaction and .20 to list an item for sale. Paypal takes another 2.9% + .30 per transaction. There is an excellent free tool for figuring costs for both Etsy and Paypal costs at http://www.feesnap.com/etsy.html.

In addition to the two obvious costs, there are additional costs that some Etsy owners do not factor into their price models. No wonder they are not making much money!

Most of these business costs are not expensive individually, but they can easily add up to the point that they are eating to your profits, if you don't adjust your item price or shipping and handling costs to account for them.

For instance, packaging costs can easily add up to over 50 cents a transaction, especially if you use custom-made boxes, gift wrap, etc. You may also have to pay for bubble wrap, tape, invoice slips, etc. You can lower this price significantly by buying materials in bulk online. It's also a good idea to have your friends and family save materials like bubble wrap, shipping containers, packing peanuts and Styrofoam, if you need it for packaging your items. Every little bit helps the bottom line.

Some other costs that subtract from your profits: advertising upgrades, shipping overages, printer ink, shipping labels, costs to prepare your item such as cleansers for vintage items and gas costs for driving to the post office.

Another thing that you should consider is the time you spend on each item. I assign a value of $5/Hour for my time spent prepping, listing, packaging and shipping.

Your formula for figuring profits may end up looking like:

Item Sale Price + Shipping and Handling charged – (Cost of Item, Materials + Etsy & Paypal fees + Actual Shipping purchased + Additional costs) = Profit

Now that we understand how to determine actual profits, let's examine several types of price points for your Etsy shop.

There are several different methods that you can use to price your items. The manner in which you apply these methods is going to depend on what types of items you are going to be selling.

That being said, I think that the best way to guarantee consistent success is to use a model with three levels of pricing. Why? Because your shop can cater to the big fish who want to spend a wad of cash in your shop with high-priced goods, and you can also offer low-priced items so that people can sample your goods before buying your big ticket items.

The most important tier is the high price point. This is where your real money-making items are housed. In some shops, this is 80% of their inventory. In other shops, such as jewelry findings shops, there may only be 20% of the inventory's items in the high-price level. But, it important to have some items that you can offer buyers at a high-price. This can be accomplished by creating collector's packages, bundling multiple items, or using high-end materials for craft goods.

Your goal should not only be to sell X number of items from your Etsy shop, your goal should be to sell a consistent number of items that are priced in the top 20% of items in your category. That includes both your items and other sellers' items with similar stock. It may take you a while to be able to produce handmade items that are of sufficient quality that you can offer them in the top 20%. You may also have to save up some Etsy sales profits to be able to afford to buy the higher priced materials or vintage collectibles that enable you to sell at this higher price point. But, you will get there quickly if you set a reachable goal and write it down.

For instance your goal for month 1 of your business could be: "I will list 10 items in the top 20% of handmade beeswax candles for sale on Etsy by the end of July."

Now, how would you go about accomplishing that goal? I would go to Etsy and search "beeswax candles". Right now there are 6300 listings for beeswax candles on Etsy. 20% of 6300 = 1,260. On the top right corner of the page, there is a 'sort' button. Sort by price, highest first. You will get a new list of beeswax candles with the highest priced candles listed first. There are 30 listings per page + some ad listings. 1260 / 30 = 42.

Skip down to page 42 by clicking on the page links at the bottom of the page. OK, we are on page 42 (It takes a minute to skip through the pages). Let's look around. The prices on page 42 are between $19 and $19.95. So, we can easily accomplish our goal! A listing that will sell for about $20 should be easy to make. Eventually, we will want to get some listings in the top 10% and make some $50 sales, but let's start with our initial goal.

Let's try to figure out what other sellers have done to be able to list relatively inexpensive products like beeswax candles for about $20. Here are several examples from page 42:

1. Large personalized candles
2. Skull shaped candles – unique shape

3. Sets of 4-8 candles
4. Candle Kits for making candles
5. Candles with unique packaging, so that people can give them as gifts

These are all examples of methods of achieving the high price point, without a lot of extra expense. Obviously, the easiest and sometimes cheapest method is to bundle a group of candles together, so that you can list the lot of candles at a higher price. What makes more sense, making 10 different Etsy listings for individual candles at $2 each, or offering one listing for a lot of 10 candles at $20?

This should be easy for you. The $20 listing saves several hours of your time, because you don't have to list 9 additional items, plus you save on the time it takes to package and ship 9 additional orders. You make one listing and save time and money in Etsy and Paypal fees and packaging and shipping costs.

Having a number of high-priced items in your shop also lets customers know that you sell high quality items and that should be one of your primary goals. Once you establish a reputation as being a premium Etsy shop, you will sell more items overall and you will sell your high-end items with more consistency.

Although your goal should be to sell high-end items for the greatest profit, having low priced items is also important. These low priced items allow shoppers to sample your goods, which is good for a number of reasons.

First, it builds trust in your brand. Customers that are happy with their lower priced purchases are much more likely to come back and buy your premium items. They may also tell their friends and family about the item that they bought.

Low priced items can also be the first step in building a relationship with a new customer. You should use that opportunity to offer a coupon for a return visit to your shop and an invitation to join your mailing list or check out your blog or social media pages. Many sellers will offer low-priced items at cost to lure new shoppers into their sales funnel.

Most sellers also use a third price tier in their price models. You can either offer a medium price tier or an ultra-premium price point for collectors and top customers.

HOW TO MAKE PROFESSIONAL ETSY LISTINGS

I have looked at hundreds of Etsy shops to determine the reasons that they have been consistently successful. There are two areas where profitable shops excel. Almost all successful shops have a large inventory with several price points. These shops also have professional-looking item listings that are consistent with the shop's brand and build customer's confidence before asking for the sale.

Let's take a look at each portion of the listing process and talk about what you can do to improve your sales and shop reputation. Again, the more listings that you look at while you are in your research phase, the more ideas that you will pick up from other shop owners. Take notes on what you like and how you would like to utilize that information to improve your own listings.

Another interesting research session would involve looking at 10-20 random listings on Etsy and then go to Craftcount.com again and look at 10-20 listings from the top 10 shops on Etsy. What do the top shops do that others don't? What would you like to include in your listings? First, let's discuss what the average listing looks like on Etsy.

Many sellers use one, possibly two photos of the item. The photos look like they are sitting on a countertop in the kitchen of the seller. The description is one paragraph long and gives very basic information on the item. Condition is described minimally on vintage used items. The title of the item is very matter-of-fact and contains only one keyword that could be found by Etsy search engines. There are only one or two tags attached to the listing.

What type of shopper is going to buy items from this seller? People that already know what they want may order from this seller, but shoppers who are browsing and comparing items before buying probably will not buy here. There are other items that are comparable in price that are presented more effectively by a more professional seller.

Let's take a look at several ways to upgrade your listings into the upper class of Etsy sellers.

Photographing Etsy Items

The average Etsy shopper is primarily visually-oriented. Therefore, your photos are the most important aspect of your listings. Your photos should stand out from the other listings in your category's list and on browsing pages.

Adding photos to your listing is very easy. Take photos with a digital camera, download the photos to your computer – you can either download to a folder on your desktop or a folder that you designate in your 'My Pictures' file. Select the photo from Etsy and upload. You can also crop each photo from the Etsy Cropping tool before moving on to the next photo.

Before we get into the nuts and bolts about how to make your photos pop, we have to first talk about the overall quality of your photos. Nothing screams 'Etsy rookie!' like having photos that are out of focus, or have other items visible in the background that are not for sale (like your coffee cup or your cat).

In my opinion, the first place that an Etsy seller should spend their money when they are building their business is to get everything that they need to photograph their items so that their listings look awesome on Etsy (and eBay). Remember, in a virtual marketplace like Etsy, the customer cannot actually pick up your item and examine it. That is why you have to provide the best photographs possible of your items to recreate the effect of holding the item in one's hands and examining it.

When you are starting out with your Etsy business, you can get by using the point-and-shoot digital camera that you already own. Some cell phones even do an adequate job (check out some free tips for using your cell phone here - https://blog.etsy.com/en/2013/top-tips-for-smartphone-photography/).

To take your business to the next level, you are going to have to get a hold of a camera that can take beautiful photos, especially if you sell small items like jewelry or beads. You can save money by buying a lightly used camera on eBay or Amazon. Sometimes, you can actually buy a used camera package that comes with a tripod and a zoom lens for cheaper than you can buy the camera new at a retail shop.

There is an excellent selection of 35 articles that covers many subjects that can help Etsy sellers to become better photographers. The articles also discuss camera features, selecting a camera, building a light box for your studio, and much more. Do not proceed with this book until you have read the articles and taken notes from here:

http://www.handmadeology.com/big-list-of-product-photography-tips-for-etsy-sellers/

The Best Camera for Etsy: Buying a Camera and Accessories

Before we get into discussing particular cameras, you have to understand that no matter which camera you buy, you will have to learn how to take great photos with your camera. The camera does not take photos by itself! You will have to take dozens, if not hundreds of photos before you become an expert with your camera.

Don't expect to take professional quality photos immediately. Experiment with the features of your camera and make adjustments. Learn how to take great photos in a variety of locations. Take photos of various types of goods.

Practice, practice, practice.

The best type of camera for an Etsy business is a DSLR (Digital Single Lens Reflex) camera. DSLR cameras allow you adjust many settings, including the aperture, exposure time, white level, shutter speed and ISO levels. I would recommend getting a camera with a Live View window, so that you can immediately see the photo that you took. Most new cameras have the Live View window, but if you are buying an older used camera, make sure that it has a window. Another thing to look for is a camera with a built-in automatic flash.

It's not vital to get a camera that has over 20 megapixels. Any entry level DSLR camera will take great photos for your Etsy shop.
Here are several new DSLR cameras that are used by many Etsians:

Canon Rebel T4i
Nikon d5200
Sony Alpha

You can also get some good deals on quality name-brand cameras with accessory bundles on eBay for $200-300.

Here is a web page that allows you to compare features of DSLR camera side by side.

http://www.dpreview.com/products/compare/cameras

Some extras that will help you take better photos:

- A tripod and remote control – holds camera still, so you don't get blurry photos
- A Light box – Click on the hyperlink for an excellent lightbox with two exterior lights and a camera tripod for $30. Also has several colored backdrops.

Photography Tips by Etsy Professionals

Here is a selection of very helpful photography tips from my own experience and some tips collected from various websites on the internet:

- The first photo is the one used to showcase your item in the largest size. Make sure that the first photo is your best one.
- Think about what you would want to see, if you were buying your own item. Take tons of photos and pick out the best 5 photos for your listing. My favorite selection is: 3 photos from different perspectives – above, front, behind, etc., 1 photo of a

person actually using or wearing the product and one photo of the item in a gift box, or in the packaging. Many shoppers are buying items to give as gifts.

- Use close-ups to highlight textures and small details in your items.

- Etsy has a fairly good cropping tool that allows you to cut your photo down to size or eliminate objects in the background. I use Picasa 3 (free) to enhance photos. It has a better cropping tool and many other features that help to upgrade photos and highlight certain aspects of your items. It also allows you to put labels, tags and text into your photos.

- Use natural lighting when possible. Direct sunlight can be too harsh for some items. Experiment by taking photos at various times of the day, either outside or just below a large window. Many sellers say that photographing items outside on a bright cloudy day, or on a clear day at dusk works great.

- You will get the clearest photos for small items using the 'Macro' setting, which is usually represented with a flower icon on the camera setting dial.

- Make your photos POP by using different background colors and textures. At my house, I have used maroon and light green colored walls, a black leather sofa, a cream colored corduroy sofa and white wood backgrounds. If you use a custom background, make sure that is not too "busy", so that your item is hard to see.

- Use white poster board or foam board behind your item to reflect light and highlight all sides of your items. Make a cheap DIY light box using the instructions here: http://www.handmadeology.com/a-6-dollar-solution-to-photographing-jewelry/

- Use white tissue paper over your windows to diffuse the light, if it is too harsh for mid-day photography. Use additional layers for more brightness filtering.

- Here is some great information on photographing clothing and the use of silver backdrops and black backdrops to highlight items: http://www.handmadeology.com/clothing-photography-tips-making-your-product-pop/

- For clothing and jewelry, use photos of people wearing the items in order to make them more appealing. If shoppers can picture themselves wearing your item, they will be more likely to buy them. Crop out the model's face, if possible. As a substitute, you can use a mannequin. Anything looks better than clothing on a hanger, or laid on a table.

- Here is a great article on how to use props and backgrounds to showcase your items: https://blog.etsy.com/en/2008/give-props-how-to-style-your-photos/

- Notice how the blogger uses creative and colorful props that highlight different uses of the item. Make your item more desirable to shoppers by displaying photos of people having fun with the item or show different uses of the item in your photos that will appeal to shoppers.

- When all else fails, take more photos. Digital photos are free! Take dozens of photos and use the 5 photos that are the best.

Writing Engaging Item Descriptions that Yield More Sales

Some Etsy sellers are intimidated by having to write sales copy to sell items. Other sellers think that the item photos will sell the item by themselves.

You will have an advantage over both of these sellers… and it will only take you a couple of minutes to do so.

You do not need to be a wordsmith to write a very effective item description. Think about what you would like to see in a description of an item that you were considering purchasing. Most buyers want to know exactly what they are buying and if they are buying a collectible used item, they want an accurate description of the item's condition.

As an Etsy seller, your primary task is to tell the customer exactly what the item is and how it works. Your second task is to describe the condition of used items. Let this sink in for a moment. DO NOT even think about selling your item to your customers until those two tasks are complete. Why? Your shop's reputation is very important. Don't risk receiving negative feedbacks and reviews of your shop by offering items with missing or misleading information.

It is definitely not worth gaining a sale or two by making your items seem better than they are, or by providing misleading item condition descriptions.

The best way that I have found to package this information is as follows:

1. A short paragraph describing the item to shoppers. What is, what is it used for, and perhaps a short statement about why the item is unique or valuable.
2. A bulleted list that includes: Size / measurements, composition, variations, colors and attributes (made from recycled materials, allergen-free, machine washable, etc.)
3. A paragraph describing condition of used items, or to describe how your item was made or fun uses of the item.
4. A link back to your main shop URL – Any Etsy URL that is included in descriptions will be hyperlinked, so customers can click on them to navigate. You want customers to stay in your shop as long as possible and perhaps even bookmark it to come back later.

Product Description Example #1:
Handcrafted Natural Beeswax Candle

Enjoy the warm glow of this 6" tall beeswax candle. Candles make a perfect gift for any occasion, as well as a warm, inviting addition to your home. Benefits of beeswax:

- *A natural, renewable resource*
- *Longer lasting than traditional wax candles*
- *Emits no harmful fumes when burning. In fact, beeswax is a natural deodorizer and air cleaner*
- *Your natural (Brand X) pillar candle:*
- *Is made from pure beeswax from Southwestern US bees*
- *Burns clean and bright*
- *Is drip-less and smoke-less*
- *Measures 3" across and approximately 6" in height*
- *Has a cotton wick*
- *Weighs approx. 1 pound*
- *Is shipped in shredded recycled paper for protection*

I hope you enjoy the quality and eco-friendly properties of your (Brand X) beeswax candle! If you have any questions, please feel free to contact me.

Visit BeeswaxRUs (hyperlinked) for hundreds of unique beeswax candles!

Tips for a Great Item Description

1. The first two lines (160 characters) of your descriptions are also used in your Google meta description and for search engine optimization. Make sure that the most important information appears at the beginning of the description, along with the title

of the item and keywords or keyword phrases from your research.

2. Make it easy for customers to find the information that they are looking for. Bullet points and short paragraphs make descriptions easier to read. Most customers will make up their mind whether they are buying the item by looking at your photos. They will read the description only to verify that the item is what they are looking for and answer key questions they have – what's it made out of, is it machine washable, how big is it? Your goal should be to tell them what they need to know and direct them to your order button.

3. You will not talk many people into purchasing item via the description – show customers that you are excited about the item without overwhelming them.

4. People will respond more to reading about benefits to using the item than they will to reading flowery praise by sellers. Give them the information, and let them buy the item.

5. Treat customers like your friends. Use 'I' and 'we', and invite them to come back and see you again. Make them feel like an old friend when they return back to your shop for another purchase.

6. Once you find a listing description that yields sales, you can copy that listing from your shop inventory and use it as a template for new listings. This saves a lot of time, as you only have to change the details and you can post a new listing.

Etsy Item Titles: Optimizing for SEO and Browsing

Etsy item titles can bring you traffic and item orders in three ways. Incoming traffic can come from either the Etsy search engine or from outside search engines like Google and Bing. You can also get traffic via customers browsing on Etsy category pages.

The question is – how can you bring in the most traffic with your item title? You are allowed 140 characters in the title. Sellers are tempted to stuff as many keywords into the title as possible, but that is not the most effective game plan. Your title must still be attractive to browsing customers. Stuffing titles with nonsense keywords turns off both customers and search engines. Both google and Etsy search engines have been updated many times to prevent keyword stuffing.

The goal is to use all 140 characters of the title to utilize keyword phrases that sound natural and attractive to buyers. Here are the most important things to consider when writing Etsy item titles:

1. Make the title easy to read and attractive – customers skim and browse titles for relevant words that they are looking for.

2. Leave no doubt about what your item is. Be clear. '1960s Bakelite Bracelet – Chunky Red/Yellow Striped Bangle'

3. Put your most important keywords first. If they are in the first three words, it is even better. The beginning of the title is weighted more in SEO.

4. Work several of your highest ranking keyword phrases into the flow of the title. Long-tail keyword phrases of 4 words and longer can be very effective for Etsy listings that usually do not rank highly on Google.

5. Vary your keywords in the titles of related items. If you have a bunch of similar lots of beads, do not use the same keywords in all of the titles and only change the color.

6. Don't use many of the adjectives that are abused in titles, e.g. Unique, Rare, Homemade, Awesome, Cute, etc.

7. Look at the top rated sellers in your categories. Do they use a particular phrase or adjective consistently? If so, use it in your titles.

8. Don't get cute and capitalize every other letter or entire words for emphasis. Customers aren't stupid. It just annoys them.

9. Try not to use the same keyword more than once in a title.

Item Tags for Additional SEO

At the end of every listing page, there is an opportunity to add tags relative to your item. These tags are actually metadata used by the Etsy, Google and Bing search engines to find your item. You are also allowed to add up to 14 Materials Tags that are separate from the other tags and you are automatically assigned up to two tags when you select your style tags (and you should always select both style tags), one tag for your occasion selection (holidays, birthdays, etc.) and one recipient tag. Really you have 30 tags available – 13 tags and 13 material tags, plus 2 style tags, a recipient tag and an occasion tag. Each tag can be up to 20 characters, so you can also use short keyword phrases or combine two keywords into one tag.

Etsy allows sellers to use up to 13 tags for each item and you should make use all of them. Each tag is another way to get customers to your item page. Don't waste those opportunities! Tags are another way for you to add the keywords that you found during your research to sell your goods.

One free tool that allows you to compare two similar tags for popularity, views per day and relevance is:
http://www.tools4etsy.com/tagwars

So, how do we make the best use of our 13 tags?

I'll give some tips about how I use my tags. First, do not overlap keywords. For instance, if your style tags are 'art deco' and 'retro', you should not use those words again in your tags. Keywords that are already in your title should not be used exactly in your tags, although you can vary them slightly and add them as a new keyword or phrase in your tags. The same is true of keywords used in material tags – don't use the same exact word(s) in your tags.

First, take a look at the tags that are trending on Etsy. These are the most frequently searched tags on the site: https://www.etsy.com/treasury/?ref=fp_treasury. The trends are displayed on the right side of the page.

- Remember, just because a keyword gets a lot of hits, doesn't mean that it is a good keyword for you to use. Sometimes, keywords and tags with lower competition can be better for you to use.
- Your shop name should be in some of your items' tags, so Google searches can bring browsers to your Etsy listings.
- Use your keyword phrases that are under 20 characters from your research.
- Plural forms of words are already combined in search engines, so you do not have to use both 'ring' and 'rings' as tags.

- Think like your customers. What are they going to be typing into a search bar to find what they are looking for?
- Be creative. Try to think of unique combinations that most other sellers are not already using, but your customers are searching for.

Let's take a look at an Etsy listing that I just sold yesterday. The listing was for a lot of 20 vintage radio tubes (from the interior of old radios), which I sold for $25. These old tubes are used mostly for art projects and steampunk projects.

For my style tags, I used 'Steampunk' and 'Sci Fi'. Occasion: Birthday

Materials: Glass, Silver, Electronics, metal, steel, aluminum, gold

Tags: Radio Tube, Glass Tube, vintage tube, antique radio, antique tube, Easter sale, mad scientist, steampunk art, steampunk supply, steampunk parts, scrap tubes, scrap radio, radio parts

The tags must have worked, as this item sold in less than two days and at a higher price than I thought it would sell for.

Some other ideas for tags: Your name (in case people search for your items, but can't remember your shop name), the name of your Etsy circle or group, colors, color + Item, item + lot (for group of items), best + Item Name, Occasions/Holidays + Sale, 1960s, 1970s, 1980s, whatever the teens are using for "cool" (like epic, right now), holiday + Item (Easter ring), Item + sale (Ring Sale, Ring Clearance).

Looking for additional tags?

Ask these questions, and use the answers for tags.

What is it?

What is it used for?

Who uses it?

What are the most important features?

When is the item used?

PACKAGING AND SHIPPING SOLD GOODS

Etsy provides sellers a number of good resources on their blog to help learn the best practices for shipping sold orders. These articles are a great place to start for new Etsians (Make sure you read the comments, as well):

https://blog.etsy.com/en/2009/seller-how-to-shipping/

https://blog.etsy.com/en/2013/4-steps-to-shipping-success/

https://www.etsy.com/help/article/3107 - US Shipping Options

https://www.etsy.com/help/article/190 - Setting up Shipping Profiles for your items

https://www.etsy.com/help/article/191 - Combined Shipping and Discounts

https://www.etsy.com/help/article/3363 - Adding Insurance for Packages

https://www.etsy.com/help/article/374 - Marking items as shipped, notifying buyers

Here is another excellent blog post on Etsy shipping and packaging: http://outright.com/blog/25-ways-to-avoid-etsy-shipping-horror-stories/

If you are a new Etsy shop owner, it is very important to understand that Etsy is not like eBay and Amazon when it comes to packaging and shipping sold items. On eBay, it's usually acceptable to package items in a sturdy used box.

Veteran Etsy shoppers are accustomed to being treated differently. Most seasoned Etsy shop owners go the extra mile to make their packaging look exceptional. It is always worth the extra time spent to make your package presentable.

Many Etsy beginners make the mistake of overlooking the opportunity to offer their items to their customers in premium packaging, because they think that it costs too much money. However, you can offset most additional costs by adding a handling cost and then explaining that handling cost in your Shop's shipping policies.

Remember, the package that your customers receive is often just as important as the item inside.

Imagine two scenarios:

#1 – You buy a handmade silver necklace for your mother on Etsy. You sold some extra items at your house to so that you had extra money to buy it. You receive the necklace in the mail three days later. You are so excited! The outer package is wrapped in silver wrapping paper with a cute bow. You know that it is the necklace because the shop name is on the package. When you open the package, you see that the necklace has been gift-wrapped, as you requested and it looks fabulous. The package is also surrounded with padding. There is a card inside the package thanking you for the order and several business cards, so that your friends can visit the shop on Etsy. What are you thinking after this buying experience? This Etsy shop owner wants me to come back, right? This shop owner cares about her customers. Her items and shop must be special because she spends the extra time on the packaging.

#2 – You buy the same silver necklace. You receive the package a week and a half later in a plain brown box. You don't know what is in the box until it is opened. You look into the box and the necklace is jumbled up in a clear bag, which has been "padded" with old newspapers. There is nothing to say where the necklace came from. Talk about impersonal!

Which shop is going to get return more return customers?

Etsy Packaging

Your packaging is another great place to establish your brand and develop customer loyalty. This should be one of your primary goals, right from the beginning. It should be part of your planning process, if you have not yet launched your shop. Decide how you want to offer your items to customers.

How will your packaging 'wow' your customers? How can you package sold items to develop your shop's brand? How much will this packaging cost and how can you allow for the additional cost by raising your item prices or adding handling fees?

Remember, one of our goals is to offer premium priced items for sale in our shop. People that buy high priced items expect to be treated like high-end shoppers and that should be addressed in your packaging and shipping practices.

Here are some minimum requirements for packaging your medium to premium priced items:

1. Brand your packaging. You can have attractive stickers/labels pre-made and stick them on the outside of your boxes. Make sure that customers know that the package is from your shop before they open it.

2. Wow Factor – Make that moment when your customer first sees your package in the mail or on their doorstep memorable. Nothing will bring customers back to your shop faster! If a customer that bought one of your $50 items sees your package and says "Oooooh!", that is great for business. That person is

also much more likely to tell their friends and family about their experience.

3. Provide an invoice inside the package, with your logo on it.

4. Enclose an additional marketing page, with a sincere and personalized thank you note and your shop's logo and URL, so they can come back to your shop. This is also a great place to add a coupon, your social media links, or even descriptions of additional premium items from your shop. You can also add a couple of business cards, magnets or bookmarks with your shop logo on them.

5. Offer gift wrapping options in your shop and items.

6. When in doubt, add more interior padding! Do not try to save a dime and end up with your customer receiving a broken item.

Etsy Shipping

Luckily, Etsy makes shipping sold items extremely easy. Sellers are provided a link to print shipping from both sold item notification emails and from your My Etsy page. All you have to do is package your item, weigh it and print out the shipping label. Then, tape it on your package and ship it.

We use USPS for shipping all of our packages. USPS has the lowest costs for almost all packages, unless you are shipping very large packages. USPS also offers free pickup. That's right! If you have at least one Priority Mail or Express Mail package, your mail carrier will come to your home or business and pick up all of your packages for free. This is a huge time and money saver. Occasionally, we even pay the extra $1 or two to upgrade packages to Priority Mail, just so that we can request a free pickup.

https://tools.usps.com/go/ScheduleAPickupAction!input.action

Here are some ways to save money on USPS shipping:

- You will have to buy a shipping scale, so you know how much your packages weigh when printing shipping labels. Here is the shipping scale that we use on Amazon (pictured below). Most scales cost $25-40. Look for a scale that has a digital display that is easy to read – the scales with detachable displays are worth the extra money, as it can be very hard to see the display when there are large packages sitting on the scale. You will also want a scale that does not have to be plugged in, so that you can move it wherever you need it.

- You can save considerable money by purchasing packaging supplies in bulk. We buy our boxes, bubble wrap, packing peanuts, tape and printer ink in bulk on eBay.

- You will want to buy boxes or containers that allow you to sufficiently pad your items to prevent breakage, but are not too large. Remember, the larger the empty box, the heavier it will be and the more extra padding that you will have add to fill the box. Sometimes, even an extra ounce or two can bump you up to the next pound and cost you an extra $1, or more. That can really add up over time!

- Always, always, always (is that clear) get USPS package tracking and confirmation numbers for each package. Currently, package tracking and confirmation are free for US First Class and Priority Mail and costs about a quarter otherwise. Etsy provides these tracking numbers to your customers when purchased via Etsy shipping and they are also available from your Etsy page under Orders > Shipping Labels.

Providing package tracking information is a very important aspect of customer service.

- It is important to offer different shipping speeds to address the needs of your customers. Most will use the standard shipping option, but sometimes people will want faster shipping options for last-second gifts. Instructions for offering multiple shipping options are provided in the links at the beginning of the chapter and on Etsy.

- You can make your packaging and printing shipping labels much more efficient by setting up a shipping center in your home or business. Keep all of your packing materials, padding, boxes and tape in one place. It's even better if you can print your labels from the same area. Over the course of preparing thousands of packages, you can save yourself a lot of time by eliminating excess moving around.

- USPS will send you free Priority and Flat Rate boxes to your location, with no additional shipping charges. The only issue with using the free boxes is that the outer box will be the boring old USPS box, instead of your fancy custom box. You can still gussy up the interior package, but using the USPS boxes will significantly reduce the Wow factor. You have to weigh the cost-benefit ratio of using the free boxes versus the return customer potential of fancier packaging options.

- Use a printer that has affordable printer ink cartridge replacements. You will go through a lot of ink cartridges while printing shipping labels. You can also experiment with printing labels on the 'Draft' quality printer setting to save ink. Ensure that the addresses and barcodes are printing clearly if you use the Draft setting, or your package may not be delivered.

- You can print International USPS shipping labels via Etsy Shipping and your customs forms are automatically completed. I have found that the packages are usually delivered faster than the International shipping estimates provided on USPS. International packages can also be picked up along with your domestic packages by your mail carrier.

INTERACTING WITH CUSTOMERS: BUILDING LOYALTY AND BRAND RECOGNITION

Etsy provides sellers an excellent opportunity to engage customers and build your business' brand for free!

As creators of unique handmade goods and art, your goal should be to offer people an experience. Don't just try to sell them one item. Make them a friend and a fan of your shop. Those are the customers that will come back again and again, buy your premium items and then brag about them on Facebook and Pinterest (with photos of your artwork). Every super-fan that you get is worth more than ten single item orders.

So, how do we develop our brand and make some super-fans?

Some of this will be review from prior chapters, but the information is worth reviewing.

Is Your Shop in a Popular Niche?

It is very important to build a shop that caters to a niche that already has a group of passionate people that loves the types of items that you are going to sell. It is much easier to branch off from a popular category of items and develop your own unique brand there, than it is to attempt to create a demand for a totally new line of items.

In other words, there are tons of people who love steampunk art and creations. All you have to decide is how to use that demand to create a shop that establishes a new brand of steampunk items to sell in order to be successful, if you are interested in that genre.

How do you know if it is worth building a shop in a particular genre? Look around on the internet and on Etsy. Are there existing shops that are successful on Etsy? You don't want to have too much competition, but if there are several similar established shops on Etsy, that is a sign that the genre may be potentially profitable for you. Hopefully, you already have some ideas for unique offerings that will entice customers which are not currently for sale elsewhere.

You can also look in Etsy circles and see how many circles there are for your potential genre. It will also be beneficial for you to have other sellers to network with and ask questions to after you have built your shop.

Where else can you look to see where fans who love your genre hang out? Check Facebook and see how many Groups there are for that niche using Facebook search. How many members are in each group? Are there many websites or blogs devoted to the subject? Are there active forums for the genre? Check the Alexa.com ranking to determine if the sites are getting lots of traffic.

A Catchy and Recognizable Brand can make a Huge Difference

What makes up your shop's brand? Well... everything! Everything that customers associate with you and your shop, that is. Your shop name and logo are extremely important aspects of creating your brand. When people read your shop name or see your logo, they should think about your products and they should remember that your shop offers high quality items.

Your shop name should be easy to remember and spell. It should not be similar to other existing products or shops. If you can add keywords for search engine optimization, that is awesome!

Your shop's logo should build upon the brand that your shop name established and provide visual confirmation of what people think of when they read the name of your shop. If you are not a graphic designer, it is well worth the money to have a professional design your logo and Shop header artwork. Your logo and header will be used in many marketing communications, including social media, business cards, invoices, email, newsletters and other marketing campaigns.

Your brand also includes the entire inventory of items that you have for sale in your shop. People will assign values to items for sale in your business. What will they say when they browse in your shop? Unique? Provocative? High quality? Premium? Chic? Retro? Those high-value words add emphasis to your brand.

You, as the artist, curator and shop owner are also part of your business' brand. Do people like you after they read your Bio? Show your passion for your genre in your shop's description, in your personal bio and everywhere else that you discuss your shop and/or your sales items.

Building a Community of Super-Fans

If you want to take your shop to the next level, your main goal should be to organize a group of people who are passionate about your goods and your shop. This group of people can hang out in a number of locations, but you want them to regularly get communication and updates from you.

Your "crew" can hang in a Facebook group or business page, on Google Plus, on Pinterest boards, or in a forum. It really does not matter where you engage with these people. Choose one or two places, where you feel comfortable online and start there.

Wherever you choose to communicate with your fans, treat them like friends. Exchange Facebook likes and Twitter follows. Share their posts and re-pin their Pinterest photos. Answer questions when asked and talk about things that they are interested in.

Many experts consider email communications to be the most effective avenue to connect with fans and convert them into buyers or return customers. Think about it. When you post on Twitter and Facebook, only the small percentage of people that are online when you post will have the opportunity to see it. Of those people that are online, many will never bother to look at your post, especially if it is related to selling goods.

Now, what happens when you receive email? You have a relatively small list of emails in your inbox. You can see who sent you the email and what the subject is. As long as the sender is somebody that you recognize, you are going to open the email quite often. And, once you have made the effort to open the email, you are much more likely to "click through" to another website or sales page than you are from social media posts. Multiple sources online state that email marketing outperforms social media and paid advertising three to one.

The next question becomes, how do I communicate with a group of fans via email? You will discover quickly that it is impossible to manage any kind of email campaign without an email marketing system.

There are two options for email systems. The first option is to use free services like Mandrill.com and Mailchimp.com. Both of these sites are adequate for a short time, but they are free because they require you to accept cookies and host ads inside your communications. Most experienced email marketers quickly graduate to a full-service system and the one that is most widely recognized as the best is AWeber.com.

I have used AWeber for email marketing for over a year now. The system allows you to quickly build an email list in a number of different ways. You can build email list opt-in widgets that you can place on your blog or in emails. You can also hyperlink to your email list from inside any webpage, including Etsy shops and social media. There is a Facebook app for adding your AWeber link to your business page.

AWeber also has a nice selection of email templates to build professional letters and it will even automatically create an e-newsletter from your existing blog posts, if you choose. You can also add your own unique photos and/or your shop logo or header to your communications. This service is more expensive than other services, but it only takes several email promotions to realize the power of having a robust list of fans to send offers to.

There are tons of articles online that offer advice on how to build your list, but the most effective and quickest way to build a list is to get the opt-in link in front of people that already like you or your products.

Then, offer value for signing up for your list. AWeber allows you to design a follow-up email sequence which sends an email containing a document or link to a website to them after they opt-in and verify that they want to be on your mailing list. Give people that opt-in a free booklet about how to make crafts similar to those in your shop, or offer them a 25% coupon for your Etsy shop for signing up. You could also offer fans a free sample of your goods.

Customer Relations

Etsy shop owners may not realize that the manner in which they treat their customers is part of their brand. But, if customers associate your shop with awesome customer service, it can be the best branding and free advertising there is. Don't we all want to be appreciated and treated like a friend, instead of a customer?

Exceptional customer service takes extra time. There is no doubt about that. But, it is time well spent, if even a few of your original customers become regular shoppers and spread the word about your shop for free.

What are some things that you can do to build an image of outstanding customer relations?

1. This is super important. TELL PEOPLE THAT YOU VALUE YOUR CUSTOMERS AND THAT YOUR SHOP HAS GREAT CUSTOMER SERVICE. Don't just practice outstanding customer service, make sure that you tell everybody about it. Many beginners are afraid of bragging, but all successful businesses do just that. Don't be nervous about letting people know that your shop is one of the best on Etsy.

2. Practice what you preach. You can't tell people your shop has great customers service if you have several poor feedbacks on Etsy.

3. Be enthusiastic. Welcome people into your shop. Give customers that buy items a newsletter in their packages. Thank them with a coupon. Tell them that you would love to interact with them on social media. Whatever it takes.

4. Let your customers know that you value their opinions and offer to take care of any issues that arise. Sometimes, you have to refund orders or offer partial refunds, even when you know that the customer is lying about the condition of the item that they received. That is the cost of doing business.

5. Give customers unexpected gifts. Nothing excites people like getting free stuff. Another great idea is to offer a sample of an item that you are considering offering in your shop and then ask people to go to your Facebook page to give you feedback on the sample.

6. Offer great services, like premium gift wrapping and custom orders.

7. Use professional packaging and show customers that you care about them by very carefully padding around the items in the boxes (especially if you ship fragile or vintage items).

ETSY AND SOCIAL MEDIA

This is one of the most important chapters in this book. Even many experienced shop owners do not use the power of social media correctly to take their Etsy business to the next level.

For new shop owner, do not put off the task of setting of setting up your social media accounts until later. It is vital to your growing business to get people excited about your shop and show your unique items to potential customers. Social media is by far the easiest and cheapest way to get your shop's name and items in front of people for the first time.

Why is it so important to get rolling with social media immediately?

1. It's FREE advertising! The only cost you will have in setting up your social media accounts will be header design (more about that later).
2. There are millions of people already on the social media sites. There will be thousands of people looking for subjects that are similar to what you feature in your shop. All you have to do is find those people.

3. Social media business account setup is easy. The directions on each major social media site are made so that anybody can get up and running in minutes, regardless of computer skills.

4. Your social media sites provide hang-outs for your best and most enthusiastic fans and customers. THESE ARE THE PEOPLE THAT YOU WANT TO KEEP ENGAGED. Different types of people prefer to spend time in different social media sites, so it is beneficial to offer a variety of social media locations for them to visit and interact with you and other fans. There are a ton of Etsy shoppers who like the visual stimulation of Pinterest. Others prefer the no-nonsense brevity of Twitter. Of course, most people these days are on Facebook, so you have to have a Facebook presence for your business.

I recommend that you determine how much time you are going to spend on each social media site each week. It is very easy to get sucked into spending too much time on social media sites, when you should be building your Etsy shop or getting new items listed.

We all have social media accounts, so you know how it goes. You intend to "just stop in" and see what's going on with your Facebook peeps. The next thing you know, you've spent an hour chatting with a friend or doing those annoying "Who am I" tests. Sweet, I answered 14 questions and they say that I'd be Snow White, if I were a Disney character!

When you are starting out, I would say that one hour a week for each site should suffice. Later, you may wish to extend your time to two or three one-hour blocks per week, depending on the amount of interaction that you are receiving from fans. You can also choose your most effective social media channel and spend an extra hour there and reduce the other channels accordingly.

The important thing is to actually assign a time slot and stick to it. "On Wednesday, One hour for Pinterest, one hour for Facebook, a half hour for Twitter." Or, you could say, "On Mon., half hour for Twitter, On Wed. half hour for Facebook, on Fri., 1 hour for Pinterest." Once you set your schedule, stick to it. Watch the clock.

One excellent tool for social media organization and integration is HootSuite.com. The site is free for up to five media sites. I have been using HootSuite for over a year now and I love it. It allows you to post over multiple sites with one post, schedule posts and tweets in the future, save templates so that you can quickly re-post old posts and respond quickly to direct messages from other users.

On HootSuite, you are provided with a dashboard, which you can tailor to your business. For instance, you could set it up to see posts and tweets from your friends and followers, your own posts and tweets, your new followers and new direct messages. Instead of wasting time visiting all of your social pages, you can hop on HootSuite and check them all at the same time. I bookmarked my

HootSuite dashboard and put it on the top of my Chrome bookmark bar, so I can get to it with one quick click.

Once you have set a schedule, the next question usually becomes... what do I put on social media?

This is what you DON'T want to do:

- Do NOT bombard your fans and customers with photos of your personal life. You do not want your Facebook business page to be an extension of your personal page. Keep your pages centered on your Etsy business. It's good to provide the occasional post about what's going on in your life (especially if it affects your Etsy shop). Your fans want to know who you are, but will leave your social media pages if you post a bunch of crap about your kids or pets.
- Do NOT post only advertisements for your sales items or your Etsy shop. Your fans and customers go to social media sites to interact with you and other fans of your shop or subject matter. They don't go to those sites to be spammed with ads. Would you like to see another Etsy seller's ads on YOUR Facebook or Twitter account three times a day? You'd drop that Follow like a bad habit.
- Do NOT forget about your fans and customers. Don't ask them to follow you and then forget to post anything for weeks at a

time. People are on your social media sites to interact. If they don't get anything of value for a while, they will leave.

The Best Social Media Posts for Etsy Businesses

So now that we know what not to post, what are some ideas for keeping fans engaged and coming back to your social media channels for more? Put yourself in the shoes of one of your fans. That should be easy to do, as you are also a fan of the subject matter in your shop. Otherwise you would not be selling what you sell, right?

Of course, one of the main reasons that we started our social media pages for Etsy is to sell our items. But, we have to be careful about how we offer items to fans. We cannot cram the items down their throats. We cannot keep posting simple ads over and over again. So, how do we get people to buy our goods, without making them uncomfortable?

As part of our discussion on branding, we talked about the importance of treating people like friends and not sales targets. This is even more important on social media sites, as people already see tons of spam ads each day. They do not want to see more in their favorite hang-out area.

Etsy provides very easy avenues for sharing new item listings with your Facebook and Twitter accounts. There is nothing wrong with sharing several of your new items on your pages. BUT, make them personal. Post a comment under each one on Facebook, or send a second tweet on Twitter. For example, "Hello friends! Here is the newest addition to your shop name. We got the inspiration for the item from blah, blah, blah..." – you get the point. Don't just spam your peeps.

We are going to talk about the specifics of each social media site in this chapter, but here are some general ideas for posts that will keep fans engaged. Keep your posts as diverse as possible, while staying focused on your subject matter.

The goal is to promote your products and shop to people without them realizing it.

1. The number one rule of social media is to engage your fans and interact with them. When people post personal accomplishments, congratulate them heartily. If they discuss a topic, offer your opinion. Respond to as many posts and tweets as possible and make them personal. Not only will the person you are responding to appreciate it, but other fans will also notice that you care about other people.

2. The best advertisement is to get customers and fans to post their own photos of them using or wearing your products! Encourage people to leave review or post photos with your items in them. Offer a 50% coupon for posting photos, or hold a contest for the fan with the best photo. Make the prize enticing.

3. People love "behind the scenes" photos and anecdotes, but keep them short. Don't write a book. Pinterest is great for these types of photos. You can provide a link back to your shop in the comments section. Facebook fans also enjoy these photos and they only take a couple of seconds to post. Post photos of you making your items, partially completed crafts, vintage items before they are prepped for sale, a photography session, or anything else people might be interested. Provide a short blurb about what is going on in the photo.

4. Short history lessons related to your subject matter with vintage photos can be very interesting to fans and start discussions.

5. Ask your followers questions. What new product would they like to see? What is their favorite existing product? How are they using your product in their homes? It's even better if your followers post their own photos.

6. Network with other sellers. Provide recommendations on other shops to your followers and have the other seller do the same for yours. This works best if you are not direct competitors, but their subject matter is similar to yours. Always post photos – Etsy shoppers are very visual people.

7. Post "extreme close-up" photos of one of you items and have people guess what the item is. Give them a link to your shop, so they can look around and try to find the item in the close-up photo. This is a GREAT gimmick. It gets people back into your shop and browsing.

8. Consistently post photos of you and/or your assistants with your products over time. You want people to feel like they know you. Make sure that there are lots of happy, smiley photos. People like that.

9. One way to make some quick sales is to post seasonal offers, such as Christmas and Valentine's Day sales. These posts work even better if you make them exclusives for social media followers. Everybody loves a sale. Just do not make them too frequent and make them good deals.

10. Hype new products by posting release dates and posting photos of partially finished products. Get people excited. This works really well, if the items are new editions of a numbered product line, or they are seasonal releases such as an annual Christmas ornament that you release only once a year.

Visit your social media sites and page down through old posts. You want variety. You also want to visually stimulate your followers with original and/or vibrant photos. We want people to come back to our sites because they have developed a relationship with us and other fans on the site. When you look at your prior posts, do you feel like you are valued as a person and not just a sales target?

Again, you want your social media pages to be part of your Etsy shop's brand. The best way to accomplish the visual correlation is to have the same designer create all of your headers. I used Fiverr.com and paid $20 to have the same graphic designer make my Etsy shop header design and then use that same image by resizing it for my Pinterest photo and Facebook and Twitter business page headers.

Make sure that you use create a business page for each of the "Big 3" using your Etsy shop name (or as close to it as you can, if somebody else is already using your shop name). You should launch social media business pages on Facebook, Pinterest and Twitter immediately after you build your shop and have a small inventory of items listed. All of your business pages should look and feel like your Etsy shop. Cross promote your business pages by posting links on the other pages. For instance, announce your new Twitter business page on Facebook and provide a link. "We'd love to see you on our new Twitter page! Please Follow us on Twitter by visiting us at (your Twitter URL here)."

You should also be consistent with how you interact with your customers. Use the same enthusiastic language that you use in your shop, in item descriptions and inside product packages on your social media pages. Use the same lingo and keep the same tone across all of your social media outlets.

Pinterest for Etsy Sellers

Quite simply, Etsy and Pinterest is a match made in heaven.

Pinterest is the ideal platform for showcasing the handmade and vintage items from Etsy shops. Why? Both Etsy and Pinterest put a huge emphasis on visual stimulation. Your professional-looking images of your sales items will look awesome on Pinterest boards. Pinterest also caters to users who are looking to buy items much more than Facebook and Twitter do. Pinterest users are already shopping. All you have to do is get your beautiful items in front of them.

Pinterest and Etsy also share a common core user group. The primary users on the two sites are almost identical. Both groups are dominated by creative female mothers. Over 68% of Pinterest's users are women and the primary age group is 25-45. A whopping 28% of its users have a household income of over $100K. You should already understand why Pinterest is such a great tool for Etsy sellers. As a matter of fact, one of the primary reasons that Pinterest was created was to provide an outlet for artisans to showcase their crafts and artwork!

Pinterest has also grown tremendously in recent years. Between 2011 and 2012, the number of Pinterest users grew by over 1200%! This is one horse that you want to hitch your wagon to.

Another reason that Pinterest is effective for selling Etsy goods is that users stay on the site for longer periods of time, which allows people to see more of your goods (Etsy averages 15.8 minutes on site per user, where Facebook averages 12.1 minutes and Twitter averages only 3.3 minutes).

What are we waiting for? Let's get pinning!

Start by going to Pinterest for Business (http://business.pinterest.com/en/setup) and following the easy instructions to get your business page active. You will see a link to 'Verify your Website' on Pinterest. This is only for analytics and does not affect your business page. Currently, Etsy shops cannot be verified on Pinterest. You have to have a website or blog set up outside of Etsy to connect it to Pinterest (this is optional).

Remember:

- Use your Etsy header art, or a portion of it as your Pinterest photo. Crop it, or have someone on Fiverr do it for $5.
- Use your shop name as your Pinterest name - if you can add a keyword that is even better for SEO.

Some Etsians pin their Etsy listings on their personal pages. This is not recommended for several reasons. First, Pinterest's Terms of Service prevents selling items from personal page. You risk suspension by posting goods for sale on your personal page. Secondly, with a business account you can add your shop name for branding purposes. After you have set up your business page, you should edit your profile by clicking on the pencil in the bottom right corner of your header or clicking on your user name in the top right corner of the page and clicking on Settings.

Your 'About Me' section will appear in your page header right below your Pinterest business page name (which should be the same as your Etsy shop name + Keyword – you get 200 characters). This is an excellent spot to offer a brief summary of your Etsy shop, what you sell, etc. This section is also searchable by Google, so adding a couple of more keywords helps with traffic! Example: If you sell birdhouses on Etsy, your 'About Me' might say "Over 500 Unique and Wooden Birdhouses Built with Pride and Love, since 1987. Custom Built Birdhouses Available". Try to work in a couple of keyword phrases, but you want it to still be attractive and not sound like a sales pitch.

Next, add your location. This helps with Google search results. People near you will be more likely to find your Pinterest page in Google and Pinterest searches.

Check your photo. It should be clear and vibrant. Photos are cropped to 165 x 165 pixels. When in doubt, have a professional do it for $5 on Fiverr.

Check your email settings. How often do you want to be notified? Look at your privacy settings. You want this set to 'Off', so that your profile can be discovered via Google searches. You can also add your shop URL under Website. It cannot currently be verified, but it will show up if people look at your profile on Pinterest.

Last, but certainly not least, link your social media pages to your Pinterest business page. You can link Facebook, Twitter and Google+, so that you can share your Pinterest pins as posts or tweets with one click. This is an awesome functionality.

OK, now that you're on Pinterest, congratulations! Spend some time on the site and become familiar with how it works.

http://amylynnandrews.com/pinterest-tips/ - Good tutorial page for Pinterest beginners.

http://www.youtube.com/watch?v=Lia0HR_duJU – Excellent Pinterest Basics YouTube video - 15 minutes.

https://blog.etsy.com/en/2013/how-to-promote-your-etsy-shop-with-pinterest/ - Etsy training page for Pinterest – good tips.

If you are new to Pinterest, review the links above, or do a Google search for related pages. Once you understand how to pin, re-pin and build pin-boards, we will continue.

Once you become familiar with Etsy, it quickly becomes apparent that they understand the power of Pinterest. Each individual item available for sale has a 'Pin It' button, so that shoppers can pin photos to their Pinterest pages. If you hover over a photo on any page, you can see the Pin It button (the only social media link provided on the photos).

Shoppers can also pin from inside the item detail page under the Order button. Then, once an item is purchased, shoppers can pin a photo of the item that they have bought.

Etsy also makes it easy for shop owners to post their items on their Pinterest business pages. Immediately after an item is listed for sale in your shop, you are provided a Pin It link from the confirmation page. After you pin, Etsy briefly displays a page that says 'see it now'. If you click on the link, it takes you to your Pinterest page.

If you have items in your store, try this now. Pick an item from your Etsy shop. Click on the item link. Under the price, you will see the Pin It button. Pin it and then check out the pin on your Pinterest page. If you click on the pencil to edit it, you can add text comments, which appear below the pin's photo.

Pinterest automatically adds the Etsy title to the pin as a caption below the photo. You can type in the price in the comments section and it will appear below the caption, which is great for pinners who are shopping. The orange Etsy logo also appears on each item linked from Etsy, so pinners know that the item in the pin is for sale on Etsy.

You can really take a giant leap and become an elite Etsy seller by having a large presence on Pinterest. Remember, Pinterest users are shoppers. They spend 3X more than Facebook and Twitter users on average.

Still, most Etsians do not fully take advantage of Pinterest. The shop owners that do are often in the top 5% of sellers on Etsy. People think that it's difficult to market on Etsy, but it is really simple. The only thing that is difficult is taking great photographs and anybody can learn to take good pictures with practice.

Here are the steps that you must take to develop a high-profile Pinterest presence:

1. Make your Pinterest page look professional. We have already discussed setting up your photo and About Me sections of your profile. Make sure that all of your Boards have your best photos displayed.
2. Have a well-organized page. It is important to have a variety of boards on your page. Each board should have a title that tells pinners exactly what type of pins are on it. Keyword phrases in the board titles will enable people to find them via Pinterest and/or Google searches. For most Etsy sellers, Pinterest boards are built for each category of their items.

3. Have lots of pins. Give pinners a lot of quality pins to look at and they will be much more likely to re-pin your pins, share your boards and follow you.

4. This is the biggie! ONLY PIN QUALITY PHOTOGRAPHS! I can't say this clearly enough. Make sure that your Etsy listings have awesome photos, so that they can be pinned on Pinterest. If you don't have many good photos yet, re-pin other pinners' best photos of items closely related to yours. You want your boards to look amazing, not just OK. If your own pictures are just so-so, or even if they are just a touch blurry, DO NOT PIN THEM.

5. Get lots of followers and re-pins. Most of these will come naturally as a result of having an outstanding page and great boards. You can jumpstart the process by re-pinning lots of other pinners' pins and following them. Following boards related to yours will usually result in that person following you back.

6. Network with other Etsy sellers. You can get a lot of traction for your Pinterest page by connecting with other sellers on Etsy circles or in other social media sites like Facebook. Most will like and re-pin your items if you do the same for them. You can also send your pins and boards to other Pinterest users. There is a link at the top of both pins and boards that says 'Send >'.

Pretty easy, right? Right. Let's talk a little bit more about how to organize your Pinterest page with boards.

Boards basically allow you to divide your Pinterest page like aisles in a supermarket. That way, you can organize your pins by subject, display a certain group of pins to a particular group of people, organize your products by price points or seasonal interest and build your brand by offering boards like 'In the Shop' or 'Behind the Scenes'.

Let's say that you sell Loom Band Jewelry (my sons' favorite, right now). You want the names of your boards to be both functional and enticing, if possible and include keywords. Here are the boards I would initially create for my Pinterest page:

Fun with Loom Bands – Photos of smiling people making loom band projects

How to Make Loom Band Jewelry – photos of various stages in the creation of loom band jewelry

Holiday Loom Band Jewelry – organized by color – red/green for Christmas, etc.

Vibrant Loom Band Necklaces

Loom Band Bracelets for You

Awesome Loom Bands for Kids

Custom Loom Band Projects

Trending Loom Band Arrivals – for your new releases

Clearance Rack Loom Band Jewelry

You get the point. Differentiate your products by placing them in boards. Have one board for your premium items. You may have a board for a specific holiday or season. Boards that display your new products and sale products also get a lot of re-pins.

Make sure that you have boards that are not just about your products. Creative pinners love boards about making art and craft projects. Those types of boards also allow pinners to feel like they know you a little bit.

Here are some tips to post great pins that will get re-pins from others and your boards followed more often by pinners:

1. Post clear, professional-looking photos. Use the tips in the photography section. Use tripods when taking pictures, so they are crystal clear. Use good lighting. Re-name your photos' file names after you upload them to your PC for better SEO. Assign them a file name related to the subject matter and include the targeted keyword. Do not use a photo with the default 'IMG_201' label that your camera assigns, for example.

2. Vertical pins stand out more than square pins. According to a recent study, the optimal size is 736 x 1128 pixels, or about 10.2" wide x 15.7" tall. You should use images that are at least 300 pixels wide for your products and 736 pixel wide graphics for more visibility.

3. Keep your description to 200 to 300 characters long. Studies have shown that descriptions of slightly more than 200 characters are re-pinned most often. The pins should include some creative and enticing descriptive text with keyword phrases. Don't make the pin so tall that it is annoying.

4. Keep the focus on the subject of the photo and crop out extraneous background clutter with a photo editor. PicMonkey (http://www.picmonkey.com/) is a free photo editor that does a respectable job and you don't have to download anything to your computer.

5. People are drawn to photos of other people having fun. Include photos of people using your Etsy items on your Pinterest boards. Photos of you making the products will also be re-pinned.

6. Use vibrant colors. This could be your subject's colors, or the bright color could be added into your backgrounds.

7. Experiment with black and white and sepia settings for dramatic contrast to your other vibrant color pins.

Here is an outstanding post on Pinterest marketing and page design- http://blog.hubspot.com/blog/tabid/6307/bid/34042/The-Marketer-s-Guide-to-Pinterest-SEO.aspx

Here is a nice article on taking great Pinterest Photos: http://www.themogulmom.com/2012/06/pinterest-worthy-photos/

Discussion on image sizes for Pinterest:

http://freshtakeoncontent.com/pinterest-image-sizes-dimensions/

For more details on connecting Etsy and Pinterest, check out the 65 page book How to Sell on Etsy with Pinterest.

Facebook for Etsy Sellers

Facebook can also be a very effective social media site for Etsy sellers. One advantage is that you are probably already familiar with Facebook, the site's etiquette and how to post various types of content. All you have to do is set up a Facebook fan page for your Etsy business and you are off and running.

Start here: https://www.facebook.com/pages/create/

Choose from one of the six categories of fan pages. You will enter the name of your page. Connect your Facebook page to your Etsy shop brand by using your shop name for your Facebook fan page name. Add the most applicable keyword phrase to your shop – 'Aladdin's Castle – Homemade Brass Lamps on Etsy'.

Next, you set up your fan page. This is where you should be striving to add in as much SEO keywords as you can, while still sounding natural to potential human visitors (as opposed to search robots and web crawlers). Besides the shop name, you can also add keywords and phrases into your About section, in your Descriptions and in the file names of your photos.

You can add a website URL, so make sure to add the home page URL from your Etsy shop there.

There are several areas where the design of your Facebook fan page can project your brand and personality to your visitors.

1. The Facebook Cover image is huge (851 x 315 pixels). It is the first thing that you see on any Facebook fan page, so make sure that your cover is great. Do NOT make the cover yourself, unless you are a graphic designer. When giving instructions to your designer, provide them with your Etsy shop header and ask them to integrate it into your Facebook cover. If you can add images of your items or making them, so much the better. The most important thing is that your Etsy shop name has to be very clear on the header. Don't clutter it up with extraneous background images. The best logos and business page headers are fairly simple.

2. Your Profile Picture is very important, as it is also used beside every post on your newsfeed. The profile pic has to work well in both medium and tiny sized images, as the post image is only about a half an inch square. The profile picture image that appears in the bottom left corner of your Cover is 160 x 160

pixels, but should be 180px before it is uploaded. There are many designers on Fiverr.com that will design both your cover and profile pic together for only $5.

3. Your 'About' blurb is posted directly below your cover and profile pic. While the text is fairly small, you can still engage your visitors and add keywords by talking about your creative process and quality products.

4. Next to the About blurb is your Apps section. You can only have four visible app buttons, which appear horizontally across the page. The first app from the left is always your Photos App. The last photo that you post in your newsfeed is always the photo displayed as your App image. This can be a great place to advertise your Etsy promotions or new arrivals. Just post a photo that has 'HOT' or 'TRENDING' across it, using PicMonkey.com or PhotoShop and it will appear at the top of your Facebook page in the Apps applet. Another App image that visitors always look at is the number of Likes your fan page has, which is indicated with a "thumbs up" logo. That only leaves you with two logos that are visible on your page. Any other apps that you add will only be visible if visitors click on the tiny + button in the App section. Very few visitors will open your additional apps, so make sure the remaining two apps that you select are your "money makers". We will talk more about apps shortly.

5. Your Newsfeed is the main portion of your fan page. This is where your posts are visible to your visitors and where people

can post comments and interact with you. You want to provide stimulating discussions and photos in your newsfeed in order to keep followers engaged while they view your sales content. You do not want your visitors to see more than two sales pitch posts in a row. Show them that you care about them, ask questions, offer them contests, talk about your creative processes and give them tips on making handmade crafts. Provide value in your newsfeed and your Followers will return. Highlight a couple of important or popular posts and they will remain on the top of your newsfeed and be read by most of your visitors.

6. After you have made a couple of posts, the rest of your page will rarely be seen. At the bottom of the page, there is a timeline, which I don't bother updating as nobody ever sees it.

Nothing measures the status of your business more than the number of Facebook likes on your fan page. People will not check the Alexa ranking of your website or go to your Pinterest or Twitter pages to see how many followers you have there. But, many people will go to your Facebook page to see how many Likes you have. Not only that, but if you have a fair amount of Likes, say 200, you are much more likely to get additional likes. People don't like being trailblazers. Most people are followers. So, you need to have Facebook likes to receive more Facebook likes – an interesting conundrum, eh?

You can "cheat" and buy organic Facebook likes on Fiverr.com. Many Facebook fan page owners have done just that. Your only other option is to slowly build Likes over time. You can swap likes in Facebook groups to gather Like momentum a bit quicker.

You can also download Facebook Like buttons to place on your websites, blogs and place inside your email communications (your signature is a great place for a like link). Whenever you get an opportunity, ask people to first Like you on Facebook and secondly to follow you on Twitter.

Let's get back to apps. There are a nice selection of Facebook apps for Etsy sellers at the following link:

https://www.etsy.com/apps/shop_tools?q=facebook&page=2

Take a look and select one or two that you like. The Etsy Store App for Facebook is an app that I use on my Facebook fan page. https://www.etsy.com/apps/342611270/etsy-store-app-for-facebook-pages

This app places an app logo that says 'Our Etsy Store' as an App button on your Facebook page. When you click on the link, selection of your Etsy shop items are displayed, with a photo, a description and the price. It's a very sharp looking presentation. There is a free version with ads and a premium level that costs about $5 a month and had additional functions and no ads.

There are also apps for social marketing for Etsy, additional Facebook stores for Etsy and creating Facebook newsfeed ads for Etsy items. Some are free and several require a small monthly fee of under $10. However, I only use one Etsy app as one of my leftover two Facebook apps. The other app I use is the free AWeber Email list app, which allows people to join my email list from my Facebook fan page.

Twitter for Etsy Sellers

Twitter also provides some unique functionality for Etsy sellers. Although I have not received the same level of results from Twitter as I have from Pinterest and Facebook, Twitter still has its value as a social media outlet.

If nothing else, Twitter allows you to post item listings to many people for free with only one click. That in itself should be enough reason to add Twitter to your social media toolbox.

Like Pinterest and Facebook, signing up for a Twitter business account only takes a minute or two. Twitter also offers Etsy sellers the opportunity for brand recognition. The Twitter page cover is similar to Facebook. It is fairly large and everybody who visits your page sees it.

The Twitter cover can be connected to your Etsy shop header. The size is only slightly smaller than your Facebook cover. Most graphic designers can resize your Facebook cover to fit your Twitter page for a small fee.

It appears that Twitter is changing its design in short order. Today, I was offered the chance to change my Twitter page to the new design, which is constructed more like Facebook. The header image is larger – 1500 x 500px and the profile is larger, as well, at 500px square. You can also pin a popular post to the top of your profile, so that visitors can see it for as long as you choose to promote it.

Your Twitter Bio appears on your header. It is the only place to provide keywords for SEO purposes. It is also the only thing other tweeters have to look at and decide if they want to follow you. Make sure that your Bio explains what you are emotional about. If your bio is witty and/or humorous, that can help get more follows.

Twitter takes a little bit of getting used to. The quick-hitting style of Twitter differs starkly from Facebook. You only get 140 characters for each tweet, so you have to carefully plan your content. Even URL links count towards your character limit, so you may only get a very short sentence or phrase in which to engage other tweeters.

Tweeting is really an art form all in its own. It takes a while to get up to speed. It's not like Facebook, where anybody can sign up and immediately understand how to post and communicate with everybody else.

Twitter uses its own language, with hashtags and @ symbols to target specific subject matters and other Twitter users or groups. Here are some Twitter tips for beginners:

http://blog.bufferapp.com/twitter-tips-for-beginners

And here is the official Etsy guide to Twitter. This is a must-read.

https://blog.etsy.com/en/2011/etsys-guide-to-twitter/

ETSY SEO AND GOOGLE

Using search engine optimization (SEO) in your Etsy shop is definitely the cheapest and easiest way to get more people into your shop, thereby yielding more sales and popularity for your shop.

The idea is to use SEO to get people into your shop and then let your branding and quality inventory invite those visitors to become customers and buy your items. After engage your shoppers and they become buyers, then you utilize your advanced customer service practices to keep them engaged and become part of your fan base, as well as coming back to your shop as return customers.

This model will yield consistent, long-term success for your Etsy business, regardless of changes in customer demand and trends.

For the purpose of this chapter, we will examine how to get more eyes on your shop's Etsy items and Google search engine results via Etsy and Google SEO. The most important way to increase sales inside your shop is to have more people see your shop or items in search results.

Let's go through how to use SEO to your advantage, step by step.

Step One: Determine Consumer Demand

This is a review of the chapter "Preparing to Succeed on Etsy, Step 3". Review that chapter before you proceed.   If there is no interest in what you are selling in your shop, it will not matter what you do with your SEO practices.   There has to be existing demand for the rest of this program to work.

Step Two: Build a Set of Shop Keywords and Rank Them by Popularity and Importance to Your Shop

Keywords, keywords, keywords.   They are the base for all types of SEO.   Not all keywords are the same.   Keywords can be single words like 'pottery'.   Sometimes, longer keyword phrases called 'Long tail Keyword Phrases' can allow you to rank for the keyword term faster on Google because there is less competition.   Perhaps your keyword phrase for 'handmade pottery sets' gets your shop on the first page of Google for that keyword, yielding many additional views for your shop over time.

Use the Google Adwords keyword planner to develop a list of keywords.

https://adwords.google.com/ko/KeywordPlanner

Your ideal keywords will be the most relevant to your shop and its items, have high popularity and low to medium competition on Google. First, develop a list of keywords and keyword phrases that are the most relevant to the items in your shop. Then, take your list and plug them into the keyword planner and see what kind of search results you get for each keyword phrase.

If you search for keywords related to your search keywords, you will probably also come with some more excellent keywords that you did not think of that can be added to your list.

Next, merge your initial list of potential terms with the new keywords and phrases that you found with the keyword planner. Make a new list of keywords that you will be using for SEO purposes in your Etsy shop. Put the best keywords at the top of the list. They should be the keywords that best describe your items and get search traffic with low competition on Google.

Your list should contain at least twenty keyword phrases. Ideally, you would like to rank in the top five pages of Google for a selection of keyword phrases and appear on the first page of Google for at least several keywords. If those keywords have to be long-tail keyword phrases when your shop is new, that is OK.

You can also check for popularity and relevance on Etsy by typing your keywords into the Etsy search bar and seeing how many items the search returns. In other words, if you search 'Retro Clock' and you get 1100 items, you know that there are people using that keyword in their inventory items. There is good demand, but there is also considerable competition for that keyword phrase. You might look for a related long-tail keyword that has less competition, like 'Retro Wall Clock'.

Step 3: Plug Your Keywords into the Correct Locations in Your Etsy Shop

It is very important for you to help Etsy and Google search engines find your shop and items during user searches. To accomplish that task, you must plug your best keyword phrases into advantageous locations related to your Etsy shop.

Search engines only have access to defined areas of your shop, so you have to use those locations to add keywords that can allow the search engines to locate your shop and display it when people search for your keywords, or closely related search terms.

So, where can we add keywords to help with SEO?

- Your **shop name**. We have already discussed the importance of using keywords in your shop's name. This helps with both branding and SEO. You highest ranking keyword should appear in your shop name.

- **Etsy shop title**. Your keywords should appear in the title, which appears directly below your shop name on your page. It also appears below the title in Google search returns. You should add new high-ranking keywords into your title, not the same keyword(s) that you used in your shop name.

- **Etsy shop announcement**. Add keyword into your announcement, which appears on your shop page below the shop title.

- **Item titles**. Your item titles are also used as the URLs for the items in search results. Try to get the most important keywords into the URL. Remember that Google truncates your item title when it assigns your URL preview, so get your keywords in at the beginning of the item title.

- **Item tags**. This is also review. You get to assign up to 13 tags and 3 category tags for each item listing. Use them all. Vary which keywords you use for different items, so that you get more search hits for your items. Tags are used only for Etsy search engines. They do not affect Google search returns.

- **Item descriptions**. The first sentence (160 characters) is used as the meta description on Google search previews. Everything else is cut off when it is truncated. Your item title would be the Google search return title and the first sentence of the item description is used as the supporting description, so that searchers can see what the web page is about. Add one or two keyword phrase into the first sentence of your descriptions for an SEO boost.

- **Photograph labels**. This is one of the most overlooked SEO tasks. Google crawls and indexes photographs that appear on your pages. If you use your own photos, you should always assign them your own labels that correspond to their content. Plug a keyword and perhaps your shop name into the photo label for SEO.
- **Shop Categories**.
- **Your Social Media pages' titles and blog title**
- **Social Media posts – especially if they go viral**
- **Blog post titles**

Step 4: Back Link from Other Web Pages to Your Etsy Shop with Keywords

Next, find relevant blogs and websites that you can use to link back to your shop.

One way to do that is to guest blog on sites that are related to your field. For instance, if you sold Slinkies on Etsy, you could send an email to the curator of a vintage toys blog and ask if you could discuss Slinkies on a guest blog. If the curator agrees, most will allow you to post your shop's URL in the guest post author section and perhaps they may even allow you to post one of your photos or an item URL. These links provide gateways from the vintage toy blog to your shop.

You can also get links by posting on forums and commenting on existing blog posts. Ideally, these links would contain your primary keyword phrase, in order to add Google SEO juice.

NETWORKING AND CONNECTING WITH OTHER ETSY SELLERS

Etsy is unique when it comes to e-commerce sites, because many sellers on the site are very similar in their mindsets and attitudes towards their businesses. It's not a dog-eat-dog competitive landscape. It's more of a friendly contest, where everybody can get a piece of the pie if they pay attention and have some smarts.

This provides you, as an Etsy seller, the ability to make some beneficial partnerships with other sellers that can help everybody to take their businesses to the next level by networking and team building.

Etsy provides you several tools to network with other sellers. You should investigate them all and decide which combination of tools that you want to take advantage of.

How to Use Shop Follows and Favorites for Networking

Your activity feed is a collection of story updates for you and those sellers that you follow on Etsy. The activity feed button in on the top row of your Shop Dashboard, just to the right of the orange Etsy 'E' logo. If you click on your activity feed button, you will get a number of updates and recommendations for you based on your follows and shopping activities.

You can connect with other Etsy sellers by following their stores and marking their items as favorites. When you follow a shop, you will get activity feed stories when the seller that you follow favorites items or shops or starts a new treasury list. All you have to do is go to their profile by clicking on their shop page and then clicking 'Follow' at the top of the page. However, that seller must follow you for your stories to show up in their feed.

Other sellers can also "re-favorite" items that you have marked as favorites, by marking the same items as favorites from their activity feed. In other words, you mark a dress as your favorite, so you mark it as your favorite, which causes it to show up in the activity feed of another seller that follows you. If your follower then marks the same dress as their favorite, it becomes a re-favorite for your follower. Re-favorite hearts are displayed in the top corner of the item photos.

There are many ways to network by following and favorites. You can connect with other sellers by sending them messages are talking to them in Etsy teams or forums. Then, you can build your network by creating a growing chain of sellers. As you add more followers, your items are seen by more and more Etsy shoppers. Favorites also increase Etsy SEO, bringing more people to your shop.

Networking with Team Pages and Treasury Lists

Team pages are a relatively new Etsy feature that allows a group of sellers to create one page that advertises a selection of items from team members in a well-constructed format that promotes shopping.

Each team page is assigned its very own URL, so that each member can promote the team page (and thereby all of the items featured on the page) on blogs and social media pages and in emails. Each team has a captain, who is responsible for the teams' membership and design.

Etsy teams are also usually composed of sellers of similar items or sellers from a particular area, so they become excellent sounding boards for members to use to bounce ideas off of other sellers. You can also learn a lot of selling tips from experienced Etsy sellers in your teams.

For more on joining Etsy Teams, check out https://www.etsy.com/help/article/343 and https://blog.etsy.com/en/2013/how-to-find-a-team-to-help-grow-your-etsy-shop-2/.

Etsy treasuries are lists of items that each Etsy user can create to display their favorite items. These items should be a featured group of other sellers' items and should not contain more than one item from each seller.   Each treasury can contain up to 16 items.

The goal is to get the treasury onto Etsy's front page. Each day Etsy features a new group of popular treasuries based on trends and traffic, and those lists can get a huge boost of traffic by being featured.

Each treasury list has the potential to greatly increase views to items in the treasury. The lists can be shared on social media, they can appear in Etsy activity feeds of anybody that follows the members featured in the list and treasuries are optimized with SEO tags and titles so that they can be quickly crawled by Google bots and indexed.   Each treasury list also has a comment section and viewers can see how many Etsians marked the list as a favorite.

If you create a treasury, you should convo each seller that is featured, so that they can promote the treasury using social media and/or email. If you do get featured in a treasury list, you can take advantage of that by:

- Notifying your friends on social media
- Sending an email to your email list with the treasury URL
- Posting a screen shot of the treasury on all of your promotional channels.
- Sending the curator of the list a convo to thank then and offer to network and/or cross promote items on each other's channels.

- It is polite to directly link to the curator's shop, if you send promotional messages to your peeps. Share the love!

For more on creating treasury lists and the Etsy guidelines, please see https://www.etsy.com/help/article/82.

If you would like to add a treasury list to your blog or website, an easy (and free) tool to use is available at http://etreasurytool.com/etsy-treasury-tool/.

THANK YOU, READERS!

Thank you for taking the time to read this book. I hope that you enjoyed it as much as I enjoyed researching the background content and putting this book together. Please put your mind to immediately applying what you learned here in Etsy Empire. DO NOT wait until next week or next month to start!

This information is best used in concert with the rest of the Almost Free Money books.

If you have any questions, contact me on my Facebook page, on Twitter, or email me at almostfreemoney@yahoo.com. I would like to hear from you!

If you feel that this book has helped you to find new and enjoyable ways to make money or save your family's cash, I humbly ask you for only two things. #1, tell your family and friends about this book, and #2, please take several seconds to leave positive feedback regarding this book on its Amazon Detail Page. Positive feedback directly affects other readers' reviews and leads to additional orders, and the proceeds from this book will go directly into my sons' college funds.

I also have a new offer for Almost Free Money series fans (and it's a fun project). Record a short video discussing the benefits that you received from reading Almost Free Money books. It does not have to be long. The video will be used on the Eric Michael Books blog and on YouTube to help promote the books. In exchange, I will provide you with a hyperlink so that you can share it with your friends and family. If you are an author or have your own website of Facebook fan page, I will link the video to your webpage. And, I will give you FREE PDF copies of any Almost Free Money books that you do not already have, and will send you FREE copies of any future titles before they are available to the public. That's a sweet deal! Just send your video to me at almostfreemoney@yahoo.com.

SOURCES

Huff, Charles. How to Sell on Etsy with Pinterest Toplocker Media 2014.

Huff, Charles. How to Sell on Etsy with Facebook Toplocker Media 2013.

Malinak, Jason. Etsy-preneurship: Everything You Need to Know to Turn Your Handmade Hobby into a Thriving Business Wiley Pubs. 2012

Miles, Jason and Miles, Cinnamon. Craft Business Power: 15 Days To A Profitable Online Craft Business Liberty Jane Media Jan. 2013

Weber, Steve. Etsy 101: Sell Your Crafts on Etsy, the DIY Marketplace for Handmade, Vintage and Crafting Supplies. Steve Weber 2010.

ADDITIONAL RESEARCH

Since the initial release of Almost Free Money, the series has experienced rapid growth. The series now contains six volumes. Three of the books have become #1 Amazon Kindle bestsellers.

Our Almost Free Money Nation mailing list features instant notification of new book releases and free advance reading chapters. It also provides free giveaways and provides information on the hottest blog posts, without sending any spam or advertising to your inbox.

Eric Michael has developed two websites that offer free information on a wide variety of subjects that can broaden your internet selling portfolio:

http://www.ericmichaelbooks.com is more than just the home of the Almost Free Money series. It is also a fully-functioning blog with over 60 pages of information on selling on Amazon, eBay and Etsy, flipping used items for profit, selling scrap metal, locating precious metals and selling free items on the internet.

http://www.garagesaleacademy.com is another busy hub for garage sale, yard sale and flea market hosts, shoppers and flippers. The site offers many valuable tips on organizing, advertising and pricing at sales and flea markets for maximum profit. GSA also hosts a very popular page for the World's Longest Garage Sale and allows garage sale shoppers to discuss their finds and advice.

All of the Almost Free Money books (both Kindle and softcover book editions) can be found at the Eric Michael Amazon Author Page. While you are there, please stop in and say hi at the bottom of the page, link to my social media pages and a 'Like' in the top corner would be much appreciated!

Here is a very brief summary of several of the Almost Free Money books:

1) Passive Income for Life (#1 Kindle bestseller, top ten for 8 months straight): How to develop a home internet business that provides passive income paychecks for as long as you maintain your business. Make money while you sleep by building an Amazon business selling used items that you can find for under $1 at second hand locations.

2) The Almost Free Money Triple Play Value Pack: Contains the three bestselling AFM books: Almost Free Money, Passive Income for Life and Garage Sale Superstar. A great buy at $5-6!

3) Fast Cash: Selling Used Items for Profit: Learn how to find the best items at second-hand locations and build your own business on Amazon, eBay and Etsy. Contains tips for improving your eBay listings, building your brand, securely shipping items and saving money on overhead.

4) Garage Sale Superstar: Learn how to make the most profit possible at your next garage sale. Tips on organizing, advertising and pricing at garage sales, yard sales and estate sales.

5) Almost Free Gold: Learn how to find valuable gold and silver jewelry for cheap at garage sales and thrift stores. You can also learn how to harvest free gold and silver from junk sources in this fun and unique approach to earning income!

ABOUT THE AUTHOR

Eric Michael is married and is a proud father of two energetic sons. He enjoys family outings and many outdoor activities, including fishing, hunting and camping.

The information provided in the Almost Free Money series was compiled after twelve years of internet research and personal experiences developed a unique skill set – the ability to find a diverse selection of free items (or priced under $1) that could be sold on the internet for surprisingly good money.

In that time period, Mr. Michael has sold well over 10,000 unique items that were located for under $1 on the internet at an average price of over $10 an item. The Almost Free Money system has given his family the second income necessary to allow a parent to stay at home with his two boys, instead of paying for day care.

He has gone on to develop a popular website titled Garage Sale Academy that incorporates portions of Almost Free Money, and expands into other arenas of profiting from flipping garage sale, thrift store and flea market finds, as well as helping garage sale hosts make maximum cash at their sales. He also hosts Facebook fan pages for Almost Free Money and Garage Sale Academy.